"A brilliantly irre .... magic strange again. Thumper Forge brings the prankster spirit of Eris to life with sharp insight, grounded technique, and a clear understanding of Chaos Magic, Discordianism, and Witchcraft."
—MAT AURYN, author of *Psychic Witch*, *Mastering Magick*, and *The Psychic Art of Tarot*

"A wonderful mix of occult insight, humor, and practical magic that is both accessible and in depth. It is an antidote to much of the confusion found online concerning Chaos Magic and Discordianism."
—LAURA TEMPEST ZAKROFF, author of *Weave the Liminal* and *Sigil Witchery*

"The most succinct book about Discordianism since Malaclypse the Younger and Omar Khayyam Ravenhurst unleashed the *Principia Discordia* onto the world over fifty years ago."
—JAQ D HAWKINS, author of *The Chaonomicon* and *Chaos Witch*

"This book is accessible in tone and content…. From the dance breaks, practices, research, mythology, and stories, I felt welcomed, confronted, and delighted by Thumper."
—IRISANYA MOON, author of *Pantheon: The Greeks* and *Hestia: Goddess of Hearth, Home & Community*

"A dynamic fusion of Chaos Magic, Witchcraft, and Discordianism that enriches each tradition rather than diluting them to neatly fit together. This isn't just a blend; it's a true synergy."
—TOMMIE KELLY, creator of AdventuresInWooWoo.com and *The Forty Servants* oracle deck

"A quantum leap into a world where belief is your playground and laughter is your most potent weapon.... Forge will teach you to craft sigils, embrace the glorious chaos, dance on the edge of the possible, and discover that the most profound magic is often found in the heart of your good, cosmic belly laugh."
—**ELHOIM LEAFAR,** author of *Manifestation Magic* and *Dream Witchery*

"An accessible and patient introduction for the new Chaote, while also demonstrating a depth of knowledge of Discordianism that offers insights for even the most seasoned of Eris's disciples."
—**BRENTON CLUTTERBUCK,** author of *Chasing Eris*

"Forge paradoxically makes sense of chaos. The book is intelligent, thoughtful, easy to understand, and often laugh-out-loud funny."
—**DEBORAH LIPP,** author of *Bending the Binary*

"Forge has done the most delightfully heretical thing: They have created cogency, narrative, and clarity for practicing Chaos Witches and those willing to sample its catma."
—**DIANA RAJCHEL,** author of *Urban Magick* and *Hex Twisting*

"Much like the magic it teaches, *The Chaos Apple* somehow manages to be both whimsical and practical. This book is a dazzling—and yes, chaotic—waltz through the history and practice of Chaos Magic and Discordianism."
—**JACK CHANEK,** author of *Tarot for the Magically Inclined*

"The publication of *The Chaos Apple* is a moment within Chaos Witchcraft that has the potential to move the practice from the emerging or fringe of modern occult into the mainstream."
—**WASPIE JOANNE FITZPATRICK,** author of *Chaos Covens* and *Chaos Witchcraft in Practice*

"Thumper has provided a vivid and engaging overview on not only some of the main figures, ideas, and approaches, but also the primary insight that it requires ritual action in order to have lasting spiritual value."
—**STEVE DEE,** author of *The Heretic's Journey* and *Chaos Monk*

"Illuminating, innovative, and deliciously Discordian, *The Chaos Apple* is packed with novel insights and magical practices that yield tangible results in the real world."
—**SOROR VELCHANES,** author of *The Planetary Magic Workbook*

"A delicious Discordian deep dive into the cauldron of Chaos Witchcraft. Expect occult and mythic histories, meditations on the dance between chaos and order, practical techniques to enhance your own sorcery and more."
—**JULIAN VAYNE,** coauthor of *Chaos Craft* and *The Book of Baphomet* author of *The Chaonomicon* and *Chaos Witch*

"A whimsical guide to Chaos Witchcraft. Within its pages, you will discover how to conjure the inherent humor of the universe. Don't miss this wild ride through the multiverse!"
—**SVEN DAVISSON,** author of *Breeding Devils in Chaos*

"A delightfully Discordian tome, weaving magic and witchcraft with a healthy helping of dance breaks, and no matter your path, you're sure to get something out of it."
—**MOSS MATTHEY,** author of *An Apostate's Guide to Witchcraft*

THE
CHAOS
APPLE

About the Author

© B. Wycoff

Thumper Forge (Houston, TX) is a Gardnerian High Priest, an initiate of the Minoan Brotherhood, an Episkopos of the Dorothy Clutterbuck Memorial Cabal of Laverna Discordia, and a notary public. He also blogs for Patheos Pagan.

Learn more at ThumperForge.com.

THE CHAOS APPLE

Magic & Discordianism for the Postmodern Witch

THUMPER FORGE

WOODBURY, MINNESOTA

The Chaos Apple: Magic & Discordianism for the Postmodern Witch Copyright © 2025 by Thumper Forge. All rights reserved. No part of this book may be used or reproduced in any manner whatsoever, including internet usage, without written permission from Llewellyn Worldwide Ltd., except in the case of brief quotations embodied in critical articles and reviews. No part of this book may be used or reproduced in any manner for the purpose of training artificial intelligence technologies or systems.

First Edition
First Printing, 2025

Book design by Rordan Brasington
Cover design by Kevin R. Brown
Interior illustrations by Llewellyn Art Department: x, 83, 86, 212
Interior illustrations provided by the author: 58, 97, 103, 163

Photography is used for illustrative purposes only. The persons depicted may not endorse or represent the book's subject.

Llewellyn Publications is a registered trademark of Llewellyn Worldwide Ltd.

Library of Congress Cataloging-in-Publication Data
Names: Forge, Thumper author
Title: The chaos apple : magic & discordianism for the postmodern witch / Thumper Forge.
Description: First edition. | Woodbury, Minnesota : Llewellyn, [2025] | Includes bibliographical references.
Identifiers: LCCN 2025027393 (print) | LCCN 2025027394 (ebook) | ISBN 9780738775432 paperback | ISBN 9780738775524 ebook
Subjects: LCSH: Witchcraft | Magic
Classification: LCC BF1566 .F668 2025 (print) | LCC BF1566 (ebook)
LC record available at https://lccn.loc.gov/2025027393
LC ebook record available at https://lccn.loc.gov/2025027394

Llewellyn Worldwide Ltd. does not participate in, endorse, or have any authority or responsibility concerning private business transactions between our authors and the public.

All mail addressed to the author is forwarded but the publisher cannot, unless specifically instructed by the author, give out an address or phone number.

Any internet references contained in this work are current at publication time, but the publisher cannot guarantee that a specific location will continue to be maintained. Please refer to the publisher's website for links to authors' websites and other sources.

Llewellyn Publications
A Division of Llewellyn Worldwide Ltd.
2143 Wooddale Drive
Woodbury, MN 55125-2989
www.llewellyn.com

Printed in the United States of America

GPSR Representation:
UPI-2M PLUS d.o.o., Medulićeva 20, 10000 Zagreb, Croatia
matt.parsons@upi2mbooks.hr

Other Books by Thumper Forge

Virgo Witch

Disclaimer

The author and publisher of *The Chaos Apple* assume no liability for any injuries or damages caused by the reader's use of content contained in this publication, and common sense is strongly recommended when approaching all practices described herein. The material in this book is not intended as a substitute for professional medical or psychological advice. Shadow work is not a replacement for therapy. Eris is not a therapist. If you are having a rough go of things, please talk to a trained counselor, okay? They won't judge you, and neither will we.

The reader is strongly advised to consult their personal healthcare providers regarding treatment of any preexisting medical or psychological conditions. We don't know if that mole looks weird. Go ask your doctor. Additionally, the reader is advised to conduct thorough research on any plant, herb, essential oil, incense, over-the-counter pain reliever, comic book character, ancient Greek personification, or carbonated beverage mentioned in this text before actively attempting to incorporate said substance or spirit into one's physical practice. Always take precautions when working with fire, and never leave candles, charcoal, lit matches, or anything burning unattended. Fire is codependent and will act out if it feels neglected. I read that in a book.

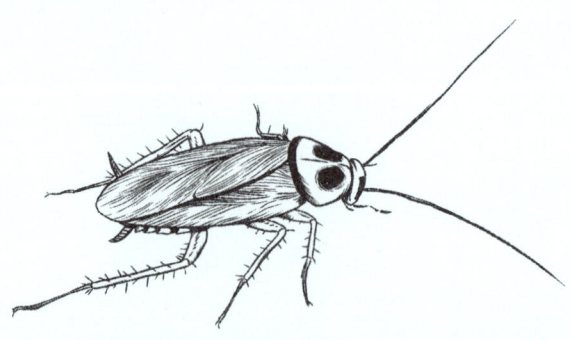

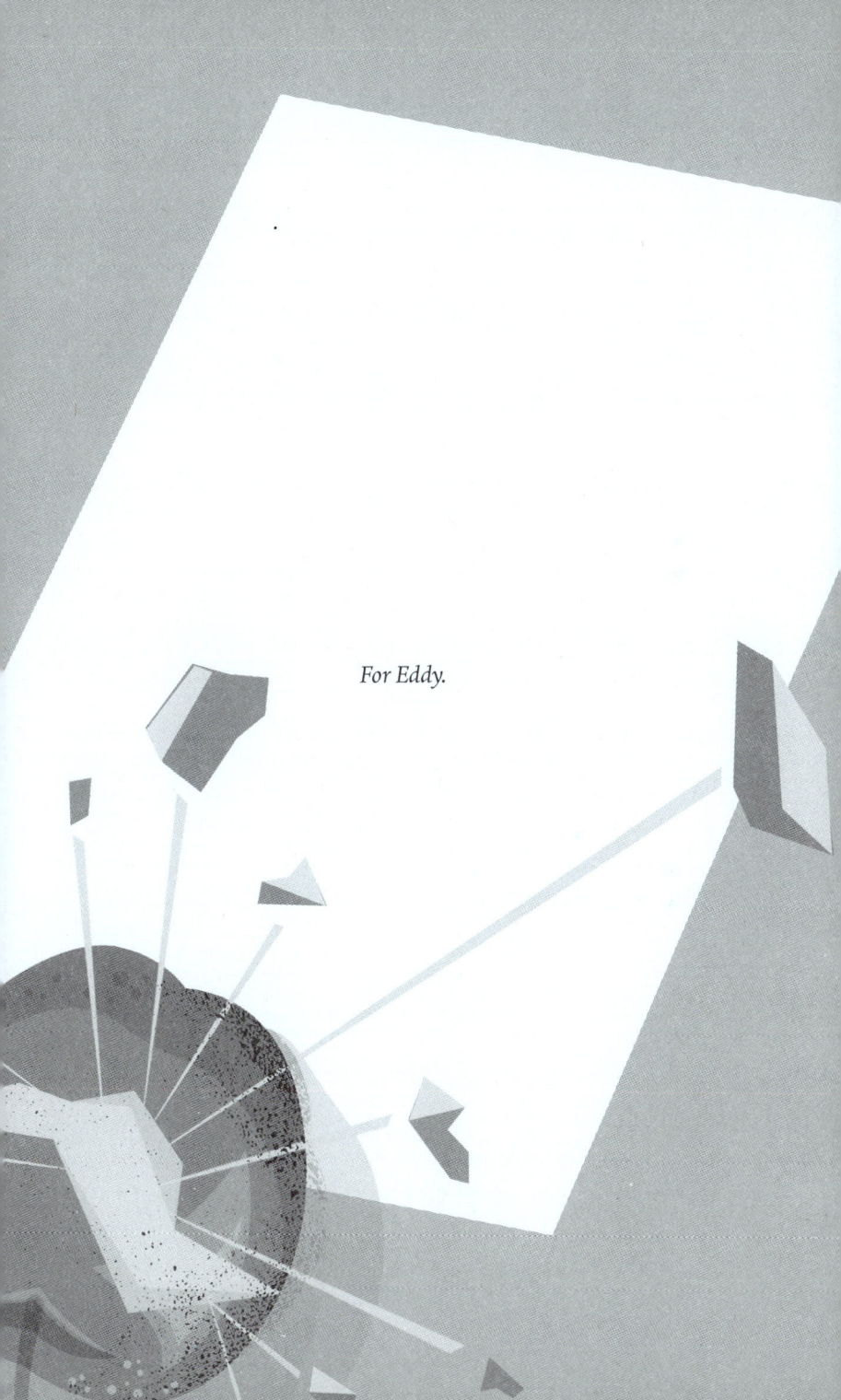
For Eddy.

Contents

Crafting with Chaos ... xiv

Discordian Dance Breaks ... xv

Foreword by Michael Thomas Ford ... xvii

Introduction ... 1

Chapter 1: The Chaos Witch Goes Viral ... 9

Chapter 2: Origins, Elements, and Eris ... 21

Chapter 3: Chaos Explained and Goddesses Snubbed ... 33

Chapter 4: Discordian Seasons and Apostles of Eris ... 47

Chapter 5: Principles of Chaos Witchcraft ... 63

Chapter 6: The Chaos Star and Discordian Diamond ... 79

Chapter 7: Sigils, Servitors, and Symbols ... 95

Chapter 8: Daemons, Demons, and Pop Culture Chaos ... 115

Chapter 9: Ethical Chaos and the Curse of Greyface ... 133

Chapter 10: Chaos Spirituality ... 153

Chapter 11: Chaos Divination ... 171

Chapter 12: Holydays and Astrology ... 189

Chapter 13: A Miscellany of Misadventures ... 209

Conclusion ... 225

Chaos Continued ... 231

Bibliography ... 235

Crafting with Chaos

A Simple Paradigm Shift ... 18

Hail, Squat ... 30

Rolling for Ism ... 44

The Five-Sided Circle ... 59

Anointings Anonymous ... 76

Customizing Your Colors ... 93

Moon Water ... 110

Cutting Cords ... 128

The Pringles® Can Curse ... 150

A Step in the Right Direction ... 167

Spreading the Love ... 186

Unverified Personal Tib ... 206

Discordian Dance Breaks

Rhetorical Questions ... 13
A Quick Note About Loki ... 27
The Gender of Chaos ... 37
Katsaridaphobia ... 51
Seeing Is Believing ... 71
Barbarous Fnords ... 84
A Better Word ... 99
A Superstitious Lot ... 121
Baneful Magic ... 141
Glamourbombs ... 161
Conversational Chaos ... 183
Chelseanacht ... 202

Foreword

In June of 2012, *Slate* contributor Dahlia Lithwick published a piece titled "Chaos Theory: A Unifying Theory of Muppet Types" in which she posited that each of us can be classified as an Order Muppet or a Chaos Muppet. The basis for this is, of course, the characters from *Sesame Street* and *The Muppet Show*.

Broadly speaking, Order Muppets are the ones who attempt to control the chaos around them. The stoic Sam the Eagle and perennial show wrangler Kermit the Frog are the best examples. Chaos Muppets, on the other hand, embrace or even create their namesake state. See Cookie Monster and Animal.

Even as a kid, decades before Lithwick coined a term for them, I knew I was an Order Muppet. As an avid viewer of both shows, I knew I was Bert, perpetually annoyed by Ernie's carefree approach to everything, regardless of consequences. I was Kermit, always trying to get people to follow the rules, as I did. I understood these characters on a fundamental level.

But the characters I loved were all pure Chaos: Cookie Monster, Grover, Ernie. I was fascinated by them, even if I couldn't let myself behave like them.

Their willingness to just let things happen instead of following a plan was disquieting for reasons I couldn't explain. It was also deeply enticing in a way that made me excited but anxious.

I have a strong memory of baking chocolate chip cookies by myself for the first time and measuring out every single ingredient precisely as laid out in Betty Crocker's *New Boys and Girls Cookbook*. And when those cookies did not come out of the oven looking or tasting as I thought they would, I was absolutely confounded.

"But I followed the recipe!" I wailed.

"It's not all about the recipe," my grandmother informed me. "All kinds of things can go wrong with baking. That's just how it is."

This was not the reassuring message she thought it was. It was deeply upsetting to ten-year-old me. What was the point of having recipes if they didn't turn out perfectly every time?

Later, I would ask myself the same question about the Christian faith in which I was raised. For years, I'd been told that if I followed a set of rules exactly, I would be happy. If I didn't follow them, or tried to bend or break them, I would be unhappy. Worse, upon my death, I would experience unending torment.

Eventually, I realized that the people telling me what rules to follow were themselves not following them. Or even if they were, they didn't seem particularly happy. Something, I concluded, was wrong with the methodology.

You would think that once I discovered the world of magic, I wouldn't apply the same way of thinking to it. But old habits die hard, and for a long time I sought out a path that would explain things clearly and provide ways of working magic that guaranteed results.

I was at least experienced enough to understand that it wasn't all just about saying the right words, making the right gestures, or using the right ingredients. Still, I thought there should be an approach that worked reliably if I applied its rules. Again, I was disappointed to discover that attempting to impose order on magic didn't work. At least, not for me.

Enter, Chaos.

A few years ago, I reached a point where I was worn out by the magical world. At the same time, I became very interested in the concept of trying to work with the genius loci of the place in which I live. As part of this work, I crafted a clay figure of how I see the spirit of this place and placed it on the table I use for magical stuff. Not long after, I found myself wanting to add another figure to it, a carved wooden representation of the Slavic god Veles. Over time, I added more figures. A ceramic statue of commedia dell'arte character Punch and the Norse god Freyr. A figurine based on Swedish illustrator John Bauer's depictions of trolls and a little plastic Papa Smurf. A chipped alabaster smoking fisherman my husband found at a flea market and brought home saying, "I don't know why, but I think he belongs with your other statues." And he did.

I call these figures the Council. At first glance, they have nothing in common. They come from different pantheons, or no pantheons at all. In some cases, they represent ostensibly opposing forces. Anyone looking at them on the table would likely assume they're simply a collection of figurines, perhaps placed there randomly while awaiting dusting.

To me, what they are is a visual representation of Chaos Witchcraft—seemingly disparate forces working together to achieve results. How they do this, and how I work with them, could be a whole book itself. But this is Thumper's book, so I want to talk about them now.

I have known Thumper for more than fifteen years, before they were Thumper (although they were always Thumper; they just needed someone to point it out), before they were writing about Chaos Witchcraft (although they were always a Chaos Witch; they just needed someone to point it out). They have always been a Chaos Muppet, bouncing from idea to idea, plan to plan, seemingly without any real direction. And yet, there has always been a direction, even when it wasn't obvious, and that direction has been bringing them inexorably to the writing of this book.

I will let them speak for themself, because they're good at it and don't need my help. What I will say is that like all the strongest magical workings, this one is manifesting at exactly the right time. As I write this, in the first months of 2025, the world appears to be on fire. The news seems to be nothing but dire. All around us, things look to be out of control.

This is Chaos Witchcraft at work on a massive scale. It's the universe being tumbled and spun around at a dizzying pace because it's out of balance. And this is disorienting for many people, particularly those who wish things worked in an orderly, predictable fashion. As we see daily, a whole lot of us are searching for ways to stop what's happening, to reverse it, to bring everything back into balance.

Well.

I suggest that Chaos is exactly what we need right now, that in fact everything has led to this point. And learning to work with Chaos, and with its attendant magic, is what is going to lead to the transformation we need on both the personal and the global levels.

Not that Chaos is relevant only in times of turmoil. The world will not always be on fire. But Chaos will always be relevant, and knowing how to work with it can lead to all kinds of adventures, not to mention results. It's very easy to dismiss the concept of Chaos Witchcraft as something ridiculous, invented as a way of saying, "Nothing matters!" Rather, it's a way of acknowledging that, often, the way to achieve what needs to be achieved is to let go of trying to control it.

If you're an Order Muppet like I am, this may be a frightening proposition. And even if you're a Chaos Muppet who revels in disorder and in breaking the system just for the fun of it, you likely have a lot to learn about what Chaos actually is and how to work with it effectively.

Now go on. Get to reading. There's a lot to talk about.

—Michael Thomas Ford

Author of *The Path of the Green Man* and (as Isobel Bird) the Circle of Three series

Introduction

So there I was, lying naked on a massage table, wearing LED goggles that pulsed rhythmic patterns of light into my eyes. Vaguely Middle Eastern trance music laced with monaural beats pumped in the background as I concentrated on visualizing and charging a psychic sigil, while my buddy Chester performed biofield tuning work around me and led me through controlled breathing exercises.

"Tell me again what we're doing?" I asked.

"Chaos Magic," Chester replied.

At that point in my life, I was dimly aware of the existence of Chaos Magic, but I knew very little about it—I assumed it was something in which cyberpunk goths dabbled during their off hours. Chester is, as he puts it, into the woo, but his practices lean more toward energy healing and goal manifestation, so I was surprised to find him throwing himself into something I associated with dark alleyways and dystopian futures.

My own background is rooted firmly in initiatory Wicca. I'm an initiate of the Gardnerian tradition of witchcraft, as well as the Minoan Brotherhood, an offshoot of British Traditional Wicca for men who love men. And while I've explored many other paths in the years since my initiations, Chaos Magic never quite made it onto my radar. But the technomantic ritual Chester put me through led to unexpectedly good results, and my interest was piqued.

Chester loaned me a handful of books—*Liber Null and Psychonaut* by Peter J. Carrol, *Condensed Chaos* by Phil Hine, *The Book of Results* by Ray Sherwin—and I dove right in. And the first thing I learned was that Chaos Magic is not a tradition, in the sense I was used to. Rather, it's an experimental approach to magical practice, with an emphasis on getting results. Practitioners of Chaos Magic are not tied down to any one way of doing things. Instead, they are trying different methods and techniques to find out what works for them, then trying them again to see if they can achieve consistent outcomes. And they are streamlining their practices, cutting out anything extraneous to create the most efficient route from Magical Working A to Verifiable Result B.

The Cinnamon Must Flow

To get a better idea of how Chaos Magical Theory operates, let's apply it to a popular occult practice and see what happens.

Somewhere around 2021, it became trendy on social media for Witches to manifest prosperity by blowing cinnamon into their homes through their front doors on the first of every month. People took this practice very seriously, and there were a plethora of Instagram reels and TikTok posts demonstrating how to properly engage in the procedure.

The typical approach to this spell would be to accept it as-is and follow the directions step-by-step, and there is nothing wrong with doing so. However, if you were to approach this working from a Chaos Magic perspective, you would want to identify a few key factors: the components, the *necessary* components, the limitations, and the workarounds. With all that information on hand, you would then want to determine if the procedure can be streamlined or made more efficient. Let's start with the components: cinnamon, the first day of a month, a doorway, breath.

In the original working, there's nothing saying that the cinnamon has to be powdered, so a cinnamon stick could conceivably be used, especially since cinnamon can be harmful to pets—a stick of cinnamon can be easily retrieved and put away before Spot or Fluffy has the chance to ingest it. But it's that last component we don't want to overlook: We're *blowing* cinnamon across a threshold, and breathing life into something is very much a magical act. If you're going to use an entire cinnamon stick, blow on it first, *then* yeet it through the front door.

Another alternative would be to add powdered cinnamon to a mug, pour hot coffee or tea over it, and blow the steam through your front door, which would also cover all the essentials of the spell. Either way, within the Chaos Magic current, we're not just randomly skipping steps because we don't feel like doing them. Instead, we're differentiating between what is and is not necessary to perform a given spell, and we're focusing on those necessities, figuring out how to maneuver around obstacles to get the results we're looking for.

Eris in the Machine

In researching Chaos Magic, I learned that some of its pioneers had been heavily influenced by Discordianism—the modern worship of Eris, Greek goddess of Discord—which delighted me to no end. I'd been a closet Discordian for close to two decades, not quite secretly venerating Eris in my own way, without direction. But as

I slid further into Chaos Magic, bumbling into online forums and thumbing through obscure, limited-run texts, I came across more and more references to Discordianism, and more and more practitioners who, if not in active relationship with Eris, definitely held her in high regard. And I also started interacting with people who referred to themselves as Chaos Witches, even if they didn't seem entirely sure what that meant.

At some point, it occurred to me that I should maybe write a book about that.

And this is where things got weird.

I kept telling myself I'd get around to writing a book, but I also kept putting it off. And every time I set the idea aside, something odd would happen, with the oddities increasing in intensity the longer I procrastinated. It was almost as if some discordant, supernatural force was attempting to get my attention, I mused.

And with that thought, my blog stopped working.

I'd been writing at Patheos Pagan for a little over a year at that point. Whenever a Patheos author publishes an essay, the post goes into a queue to be automatically added to their channel's Facebook page in regularly scheduled two-hour intervals. These posts are displayed with a cover photo and title, but for some reason, when I would attempt to upload anything, the post would appear on Facebook as an unmarked link to Patheos dot com, with no image or description. Clicking on the link would lead to the actual post, but there was nothing visual to encourage readers to click the link in the first place.

Concerned, I contacted Patheos and asked, "Help?" To which they replied, "Huh. That's odd. We'll take care of it right now." And then it happened to my next post, and the two posts after that, until I was bombarding Patheos with emails asking, "Why is this happening to me?" And they were writing back, "We don't know, and it's freaking us out."

Eventually, Patheos's IT department discovered an incompatibility between Facebook and the auto-scheduling software, which created a glitch that, somehow, only affected my blog. And because it was only causing problems for me, I suddenly realized what needed to be done to rectify the technical issues.

I sat down that evening and banged out a book proposal to Llewellyn. Immediately afterward, I added a new post to my blog, and two hours after I hit "publish," it turned up on the Patheos Pagan Facebook page, cover photo and title displayed faultlessly.

"Point taken," I said, in the general direction of Eris.

She didn't respond, at least not out loud. But my blog has worked right ever since, and I'm currently writing the introduction to a book on Chaos Witchcraft, so if anything, I am very glad I finally caught the hint.

What to Expect from This Book

On the following pages, you'll find information on the history and practice of Chaos Magic from a witchcraft perspective, along with personal experiences and recommendations. What you won't find is the correct way to practice any of the previous magic, because honestly, there's not one—there's just what's worked for me, which will hopefully give you the impetus to find out what works for you. Treat this book as a sounding board that opens roads: Borrow what works and leave the rest.

And as you read, you'll also be taking a deep dive into Discordianism, since that religion had such an impact on the development of Chaos Magic, primarily because Discordians firmly believe in not firmly believing in anything. In her own work on the subject, occultist Waspie Joanne Fitzpatrick submits that Chaos Witchcraft might be more accurately called Discordian Witchcraft, and I wholeheartedly agree.[1] However, she also points out that the term *Chaos Witchcraft* has already entered the lexicon, and that rechristening it would involve more effort than it's worth. Ergo, we're going to go ahead and roll with Chaos Witchcraft as well, but the Discordian mindset of no-belief will allow you to explore other spiritual systems at will. And by taking cues from the Discordian worldview, you'll be striding toward mastery of the core technique of Chaos Witchcraft, which is…

Belief as a Tool

In the eighth episode of the Netflix original series *KAOS*, Zeus confronts the Fates—Clotho, Lachesis, and Atropos—to avert a prophecy. The Fates are unsurprisingly not surprised to see Zeus, and they take a moment to explain the reality of the situation to him.

"For your prophecy to come to pass, you must bring it into being," says Lachesis.

"If you decide it doesn't exist, then it doesn't exist," says Atropos, to which Lachesis adds the mic drop: "The possibility exists, but without your belief, it cannot come to pass."

In other words, Zeus can let his prophecy have power over him, or he can alter his beliefs and have power over his prophecy.

And so can you.

The concept of paradigm shifting, or using belief as a magical tool, is probably the most unmistakable hallmark of Chaos Magic, which, naturally, means it's also the most misinterpreted. A lot of people take belief as a tool to mean, "I can believe whatever I want." Well, okay, yes, that's true. But there's a big difference

---
1. Fitzpatrick, *Chaos Covens and Chaos Witchcraft in Practice*.

between just saying, "I can believe whatever I want," and actively adopting or shuffling through beliefs to accomplish your magical goals.

In Chaos Magical Theory, it's understood that a belief is a subjective truth, and that structural belief systems have power trapped within them. If we can deconstruct or alter our own beliefs, we can release some of that power and use it to fuel our magic. This is reinforced by the Discordian concept of the catma. Whereas a dogma is couched in unquestionable truth, a catma is a transient truth: It remains unquestionable until such time as the believer chooses to question, rework, or discard it.[2]

Now, when it comes to structural belief systems, it's almost instinctive to look solely at the religions that are prevalent in existing cultures—Hinduism, Heathenism, Satanism, Christianity, Buddhism, and so on. And we will be talking about those religions and what we might unlock from them. But we can also remodel the beliefs we already have to be in line with whatever work we're trying to accomplish. Or, for lack of a better way of saying it, we can believe things that haven't been believed yet.

There's a wonderful epic novel by China Miéville called *Kraken* that perfectly exemplifies the use of belief as a tool. In this story, the preserved body of a giant squid gets stolen from the British Museum of Natural History, which, in turn, thrusts an unassuming docent named Billy Harrow into a war between various doomsday cults taking place in the underworld of London. The cults employ magic in a variety of ways to further their agendas, and over time, Billy starts to pick up on how magic works—specifically, the magic of metaphors.[3]

---

[2]. Higgs, *The KLF*, 31.

[3]. Miéville, *Kraken*.

At one point, while looking for people who can provide him with the whereabouts of the squid, Billy finds a key that had accidentally been paved into the asphalt of a city street. He also comes across a lightbulb that a restaurant employee had stored on top of a frying pan.

The next time Billy meets up with an informant, he's ready to make a deal:

"I can pay you. Put this in the right hands, this'll unlock the road." He held out the key. He held up the bulb. "And I don't know what's incubating in this, but someone might hatch it."[4]

The lesson here is that there's magic incubating everywhere, even (or especially) in seemingly mundane places.

As a Chaos Witch, all you have to do is hatch it.

---

4. Miéville, *Kraken*, 301.

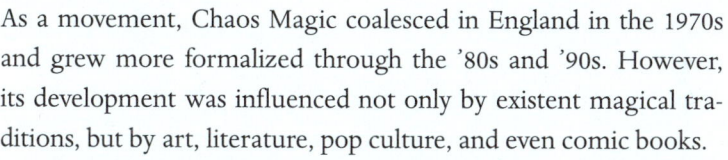

Chapter 1

The Chaos Witch Goes Viral

As a movement, Chaos Magic coalesced in England in the 1970s and grew more formalized through the '80s and '90s. However, its development was influenced not only by existent magical traditions, but by art, literature, pop culture, and even comic books.

The original adepts of Chaos Magic referred to themselves as Chaos Magicians, or Chaotes. Today, however, more and more practitioners are dubbing themselves Chaos Witches, distinguishing themselves from Traditional and Eclectic Witches by how they approach and utilize their magic. There is some nuance involved, as well as some crossover, but the deeper you dive into it, the clearer the distinctions between Chaos Witchcraft and other articulations of magical practice will be.

Creators of Chaos

The history of Chaos Magic is defined by its pioneers, along with the artists and authors who contributed to its current and paved a winding way for the rest of us to follow. Here are some of the most notable names of Chaos Magic.

Austin Osman Spare (1886–1956)

Austin Osman Spare was an artist recognized for the sexual and sometimes monstrous imagery he created. Spare's concept of Kia (or the collective consciousness of the universe) and his work with sigils laid the groundwork for the modern development of Chaos Magic.

William S. Burroughs (1914–1997)

William S. Burroughs was one of the most influential figures of the Beat Generation. Best known for his novels *Junkie* and *Naked Lunch*, Burroughs was also a Magician who utilized cut-ups as a form of divination, as well as a method of cursing his enemies.

Kerry Thornley (1938–1998) and Greg Hill (1941–2000)

Better known as Lord Omar Khayyam Ravenhurst and Malaclypse the Younger, Kerry Thornley and Greg Hill were the founders of Discordianism and authors of the *Principia Discordia*, the sacred text of the Discordian religion, which itself had a huge impact on Chaos Magic. I will be quoting liberally from the *Principia* throughout this text, so brace yourself. Incidentally, Thornley was the first person to use the word *Pagan* in reference to the modern practice of pre-Christian religions.[5]

Genesis P-Orridge (1950–2000)

Genesis P-Orridge was a nonbinary performance artist, singer-songwriter, a student of William Burroughs, and one of the original members of Thee Temple ov Psychick Youth, a loose-knit network of magical practitioners with shared interests in Chaos Magic and experimental art.

---

5. Adler, *Drawing Down the Moon*, 223.

Ray Sherwin (1952–2024)

Ray Sherwin was an independent publisher, musician, and aromatics expert who, along with Peter J. Carroll (see the following), cofounded the Illuminates of Thanateros, an initiatory organization dedicated to practicing Chaos Magic in a group setting. Sherwin's work *The Book of Results* revolutionized the process of casting magical sigils.

Peter J. Carroll (b. 1953)

Peter J. Caroll is an occultist and physicist who is credited with originating the concept of Chaos Magical Theory. Carroll has written numerous books on Chaos Magic, two of which—*Liber Null & Psychonaut* and *Liber Kaos*—brought Chaos Magic to the attention of the greater esoteric community.

Jaq D Hawkins (b. 1956)

Jaq D Hawkins is a writer of fantasy, steampunk, and speculative fiction who has also authored several definitive books on the practice and history of Chaos Magic.

Phil Hine (b. 1963)

Phil Hine is a prolific author and lifelong student of the occult, whose book *Condensed Chaos* introduced the idea that Chaos Magic could have guiding principles.

Julian Vayne (b. 1968)

Julian Vayne is a lifelong scholar of the occult who has written extensively for both academic and metaphysical publications. His work blends the Chaos Magic current with elements of modern Paganism and Witchcraft.

Wanda Maximoff (First appearing in X-Men #4, March 1964)
It feels weird to include a comic book character on a list of historical figures. But pop culture has always had a profound influence on the occult, and while the people mentioned earlier were (and are) without a doubt Chaos Magicians, it's Wanda Maximoff—better known as the Scarlet Witch—who launched the image of the Chaos Witch into the public domain.

Magician Versus Witch: The Steel Cage Death Match We Didn't Know We Needed

As it turns out, the Chaos Witchcraft current was already bubbling long before Marvel got involved and unwittingly promoted it. In a 2016 YouTube video, author and Chaos scholar Kelly-Ann Maddox explains that she identifies as a Chaos Witch versus a Chaos Magician, since the word *Magician* tends to read masculine, whereas *Witch* encompasses all gender identities. Moreover, she's a witch who engages in Chaos Magic, so Chaos Witch encapsulates the whole of her practice.[6]

Way back in the 1990s, when I first dipped my toes into Paganism, it was understood that Magicians practiced *high magic*, or theurgy (invoking spirits with the goal of achieving union with the Divine), and Witches practiced *low magic*, or thaumaturgy (the working of "natural" magic to bring about witnessable effects). These definitions were in place for a long time, but honestly, they've worn thin. They are sexist, for one thing—in the olden days, men who practiced magic were respectable Magicians, whereas women who practiced magic were untamable Witches consorting with the Devil. So, you know, kind of a gender bias there.

---

6. Maddox, "Chaos Magick Involves Drugs, Orgies & Going Insane."

Discordian Dance Break
Rhetorical Questions

Before moving on, I want you to take a moment and ask yourself a few questions. There are no right or wrong answers. These are just things to ponder as you begin your exploration of Chaos Witchcraft.

Why do you want to be a Chaos Witch?

If you already identify as a Chaos Witch, what does that mean to you?

Does a Chaos Witch need to act or present themself in particular ways?

How important is it to you that your practice be described as Chaos Witchcraft?

Are you willing to be flexible with your understanding of Chaos Witchcraft?

And again, there are no right or wrong answers here. If you want to be a Chaos Witch so you can shoot Chaos from your fingertips, that's fine—I don't know how much I can help you, but you still provided an honest answer. And I want you to focus on that honesty, getting in the habit of setting *right* and *wrong* aside in favor of what's right for you.

The distinction between *high* and *low* magic is problematic as well, since it's classist at best, and racist at worst. Theurgy and thaumaturgy are two separate things, but Witchcraft, especially religious Witchcraft, is going to employ both, so we can't really hand one off to the Magician and the other to the Witch and call it a binary.

The reality is this: Both *Magician* and *Witch* are gender-neutral terms for an occult practitioner. However, there are key differences between the two: The Magician works within a given social structure to effect change primarily in the self, while the Witch works on the outskirts of that structure to effect change in themself and the world around them; the Magician seeks mastery over and/or merger with the unseen (be that gods, spirits, or what have you), while the Witch fosters partnerships with the unseen and, in some cases, works *for* the unseen instead of *with* the unseen.

And be it known that any one kind of magical practitioner is not better than any other, nor are the previous definitions monolithic—alternative definitions with varying mileages exist, and that's legit. Regardless of the interpretation you adopt, it's good to have a clear idea of what you mean when you call yourself a Witch.

Anyway, that covers the *Witch* part of *Chaos Witch*. Let's break into the *Chaos* part.

Chaos, Eclectic, and Chaotically Eclectic

Calling oneself a Chaos Witch does very much seem to be an online phenomenon, and if you've spent any time in witch-oriented social media groups or forums, you may have encountered an occasional proclamation along the lines of, "I'm a Chaos Witch. I take from everything." Which would make Chaos Witchcraft a rationale for cultural appropriation—something that should vigilantly be avoided and that I will discuss in chapter 9—as well as a postmodern rebranding of Eclectic Witchcraft.

The big issue here is that Eclectic Witchcraft doesn't need a new label. Eclectic Witches have been around for, well, pretty much always, and Witchcraft itself is syncretic, because magic tends to find a way to survive, regardless of the circumstances in which it finds itself. Eclectic Witchcraft and Chaos Witchcraft do share some similarities, in that both are experimental in nature, and both tend to draw from a variety of sources. But what distinguishes them from each other is how they approach belief: In Eclectic Witchcraft, practices are assembled around belief. In Chaos Witchcraft, beliefs are assembled around practice.

As an example, let's say you're flipping through an old book of folklore, and you find a couple of cool spells you want to try. However, the spells include references to the Christian god, which doesn't click with you. The eclectic approach would be to remove those references and replace them with invocations to a Pagan god with whom you already have a working relationship. However, the Chaos approach might be to convert to Christianity for however long it takes to cast the spells, and then return to your original belief system once the workings are complete.

Just as a Witch is not somehow better than a Magician, Chaos Witchcraft is not better than Eclecticism: Both are completely valid approaches to magic. But while they do have some things in common, they are foundationally very different things. And it is understandable that people would get the framework of Chaos Witchcraft confused with Eclectic Witchcraft, since both suggest finding whatever works and plugging it into what we're already doing. But Chaos Witchcraft is also fueled by the avoidance of dogma (more on this in the upcoming chapter on principles), so the

Chaos Witch isn't just going to pick up techniques and jam them into an existent belief system—they're going to step out of their current belief system to see what makes those techniques tick, and to determine how best to utilize them.

The Trouble with (Comic Book) Chaos

In 1996, the movie *The Craft* premiered, which inspired a generation of angsty teens (myself included) to explore Witchcraft. And in 2005, Pagans and occultists of European descent plowed themselves into Hoodoo, after hearing about it for the first time in the horror film *The Skeleton Key*. As such, it makes sense that in 2021, there was an explosion of practitioners identifying as Chaos Witches once the television series *WandaVision* premiered, with the movie *Doctor Strange in the Multiverse of Madness* hitting screens and streaming services in 2022. Both the show and the film featured the Scarlet Witch (as the heroine, villainess, or antihero, depending on your point of view and/or charitability), whose power was consistently described as Chaos Magic.

There are Chaotes out there who lose their minds whenever the Scarlet Witch comes up in conversation, citing the blatant—albeit fictional—misrepresentation of Chaos Magic. And overall, I do understand their sentiments. But just as the fanciful Victorian concept of a Witch as a practitioner of pre-Christian religion laid foundations for the Modern Witchcraft Revival, so too did the cinematic depiction of a Witch who practices Chaos Magic result in real-world Chaos Witches.

Or at least, it resulted in Chaos Witches on the internet. Which, if anything, has moments of realness. And look, I realize that a lot of budding occultists will watch *Doctor Strange in the Multiverse of Madness* and think, "I, too, am fierce and unfettered and more than a little unbalanced! I am definitely a Chaos Witch." And you know what? I am completely okay with that. Art reflects life reflects art—some people are going to learn about Chaos Witchcraft for the first time by watching a blockbuster movie, and while a chunk of them may never get past the aesthetic or the name, a handful will head down to Ye Olde Magick Bookshoppe and start doing some factual research.

Those are the ones to watch out for. Because sooner than later, one of them will have an epiphany about using belief as a tool, and they will either warp reality or marry a robot. And I am *dying* to see what happens either way.

In her first appearance, Wanda was a member of Magneto's Brotherhood of Evil Mutants. Her mutation granted her what was described as a Hex Power, meaning that she could cause unlikely, entropic things to happen. Originally, she didn't have much control over her powers—she would wave her hands and probability would go sideways, but she didn't have any say as to what the effects would be. Over time, Wanda developed a better grip on her powers, and she started studying Witchcraft to gain refinement and control. It was also explained that she had a natural talent for magic that had been unknowingly granted to her by an ancient demon named Chthon.

For a long while, Magneto was believed to be Wanda's father, and it was understood that she had inherited her mutation from him. In the late '90s, however, it was determined that Wanda's powers, if left to grow naturally, would have been more like her dad's, but Chthon's machinations resulted in Wanda being able to manipulate magical energy instead of electromagnetic energy, specifically the kind of magic that Chthon himself employed: Chaos Magic.

In the Marvel Comics continuum, Chaos Magic is defined as an evil force powerful enough to unravel Creation, and it is considered the polar opposite of Magic for Order, the kind of magic employed by Doctor Strange and other heroic Sorcerers. As a Discordian, this is where I find myself uncharacteristically unable to suspend disbelief, because contrary to popular (and pop culture) opinion, Chaos is not the opposite of Order. As you'll see in the following chapters, Chaos is not the opposite of *anything*, simply because Chaos *is* anything.

But in order (no pun intended) to understand Chaos, we've got to make it past the first goddess to ever rise out of it.

It's time to meet Eris, y'all.

Crafting with Chaos
A Simple Paradigm Shift

A paradigm is a set of assumptions or patterns that are accepted and upheld as truth by the members of a given culture or community. If you compared a given belief system to, say, a collection of exotic plants, the greenhouse in which they thrive would be the paradigm. And just like you can move a plant from one greenhouse to another, within Chaos Magic, practitioners can move from one paradigm to another, adjusting their worldview to fit whatever work they're trying to accomplish. Here's an easy way to start experimenting with that.

It's common to hear Pagans and Witches talk about "working with" deities, which, honestly, makes me a little twitchy. I feel like we tend to say "working with" to sound proactive, when what we're really doing is worshiping, or venerating, or acknowledging—all of which are perfectly fine things in their own right.

But if we change up the language we use to define how we interact with our gods, we might notice those interactions solidifying into something more personal and symbiotic, which will benefit all parties involved.

Try this: For the next five weeks, whenever you find yourself about to say that you "work with" a particular god or spirit, say that you *walk with* them instead. Describe your relationships with your gods in terms of moving forward through the world alongside them as, if not equals, partners. See how that feels.

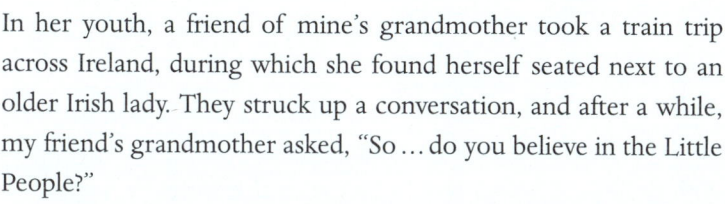

Chapter 2
Origins, Elements, and Eris

In her youth, a friend of mine's grandmother took a train trip across Ireland, during which she found herself seated next to an older Irish lady. They struck up a conversation, and after a while, my friend's grandmother asked, "So... do you believe in the Little People?"

"Oh, of course not!" the older woman replied, affronted. A few moments of silence passed. And then the older woman leaned over and whispered, "But that doesn't mean they're not real."

And that punchline really sums up Discordianism: It began as a joke, but it quietly caught on, and ironically, adherents started taking it seriously, to the point where it had a quantifiable effect on pop culture. The author Robert Anton Wilson incorporated numerous Discordian concepts and characters into *The Illuminatus! Trilogy*, which he cowrote with Robert Shea, and the British synth pop duo the KLF—known in the '90s for hit dance tracks like "3 a.m. Eternal" and "Justified and Ancient"—was a Discordian band who gained notoriety for absurdist publicity stunts. Incidentally, the KLF were also briefly known as the Time Lords and put out a song called "Doctor Who," which is played during sporting events to this day. If you've ever been at a basketball game and found yourself scream-singing "Doctor *Whooo*-oo," congrats! You were reacting to Discordian music. Eris herself has been represented on both the large and the small screen, appearing as a recurring character in *The Grim Adventures of Billy and Mandy*, as a featured character in an episode of *Harley Quinn*, and as the main antagonist in *Sinbad: Legend of the Seven Seas*.

The Principia Behind the Curtain

As a religion, Discordianism originated at some point between 1957 and 1959—nobody seems to remember the exact date, which tracks. Lifelong friends Greg Hill and Kerry Thornley were hanging out in a bowling alley, drinking coffee, talking about life, and complaining about all the confusion in the world. If one could somehow manage discord, they opined, all the confusion would be resolved.[7]

And then according to legend, everything suddenly froze, and a chimpanzee appeared. The ape was holding a scroll, upon which was a glyph resembling a yin-yang, but with a pentagon on one side and a golden apple on the other. And as Hill and Thornley stared, the chimpanzee yelled, "Somebody had to put all this confusion here," and promptly exploded... as talking chimpanzees are wont to do, one supposes. At any rate, the pair were knocked unconscious, and when they came to, they discovered that everything around them had kicked back into motion, leaving them with even more questions and nothing resembling answers.

For the next five nights, Hill and Thornley researched the symbol they'd seen on the scroll, and at some point, they realized

---

7. Hill and Thornley, *Principia Discordia*, 00007.

it was the Golden Apple of Discord from Greek mythology. Victorious but exhausted, they fell asleep, and while slumbering, they had a shared dream in which the goddess Eris appeared and spoke to them.

"I am chaos," Eris proclaimed to them. "I am the substance from which your artists and scientists build rhythms. I am the spirit with which your children and clowns laugh in happy anarchy. I am chaos. I am alive, and I tell you that you are free."[8]

Upon waking, Hill and Thornley declared themselves High Priests of Eris, changed their names to Malaclypse the Younger (sometimes shortened to Mal-2) and Lord Omar Khayyam Ravenhurst, and founded the Discordian Society in her honor, an organization that, according to them, had no formal definition. Mal-2 and Lord Omar each presided over a sect of the Discordian Society—the Paratheo-Anametamystikhood of Eris Esoteric (POEE) and the Erisian Liberation Front (ELF), respectively.[9]

In 1963, Mal-2 and Lord Omar self-published the *Principia Discordia,* a sacred text that described their worldview and included a unique Discordian mythology that explained the origins of and relationship between Order and Disorder. Although the original printing was only comprised of five copies, the book developed an unexpected cult following, and since then, several editions have been released by different publishers—the material within the *Principia* is "KopyLeft, All Rites Reversed," meaning that anyone is free to reprint it (or copy and paste a few chunks of it while banging out a book on Chaos Witchcraft).

As amusing as the contents of the *Principia* can be, not everything within it has aged well. It's worth keeping in mind that

---

8. Hill and Thornley, *Principia Discordia*, 00009.
9. Hill and Thornley, *Principia Discordia*, 00010.

regardless of how progressive they were, its creators were still two white dudes writing comedy in the early 1960s—some things that seemed hilarious back then are not very funny today. Just read it with a critical eye, as you would any other religious text.

Eris, on the other hand, has aged *very* well. Let's get to know her a bit better.

Eris the Creatrix

In Greek mythology, Eris is the personification of strife. According to the ancient Greek poet Homer, she was the daughter of Zeus and Hera and the twin sister of Ares, and because of that sibling relationship, Homer conflated her with Enyo, the goddess of war and bloodshed. On the other hand, Hesiod—another Greek poet and contemporary of Homer—asserted that Eris was the daughter of Nyx, the personification of night, and Erebus, the personification of darkness, who were both children of Khaos—the primordial spirit who existed before everything else. Hesiod also depicted Eris as the mother of the Kakodaimones, the troubles that plagued humankind, who resided in Pandora's box when not out wreaking havoc and stirring up internet drama.

Interestingly, Hesiod stated that there were actually two Erises, or Erites. One, he claimed, was a goddess of war and slaughter, akin to Enyo. The other, however, was a goddess of competition and endeavors, who encouraged humans to achieve their potential and become the best possible versions of themselves. As he wrote in his *Theogeny*, "[The second Eris] is one you could like when you understand her."[10] This ties into a description of Eris found in the *Principia*: "Eris is not hateful or malicious.

---

10. Atsma, "Eris."

But she is mischievous, and she does get a little bitchy at times."[11] Remember the blog malfunction I talked about in the introduction of this book? I can confirm.

While the Discordian understanding of Eris was clearly informed by Hesiod, the *Principia* describes her origins a bit differently than Hesiod did. While both view Chaos as the consciousness that existed before existence, *Principia* goes on to describe this Chaos (or Khaos) as masculine, naming it Void.[12]

Per Discordian cosmogony, after five eons or so (or however primordial entities mark time), Void gave birth to a daughter—Eris, who herself was born pregnant. Since she was the first being, she became the goddess of Being, and after fifty-five years, she gave birth to her own children, making her the goddess of Creation.

She did not, at this stage in the game, spawn the Kakodaimones, at least not according to the *Principia*. Rather, her first offspring were the Elements, the building blocks of reality—just not quite the Elements we're used to.

---

11. Hill and Thornley, *Principia Discordia*, 00015.

12. Hill and Thornley, *Principia Discordia*, 00056.

offbeat to bizarre, they are not, in and of themselves, Destructive: She just wants what she wants when she wants it and will make that known until she gets it.

I mean, yes, she was the one who tossed the golden apple (more on this in a bit), but it was other goddesses fighting over it that ultimately trashed the wedding of Thetis and Peleus, and it was the series of unfortunate decisions made afterward that led to war. Comparatively, if the wedding had taken place in Norse mythology, Loki would've stolen the apple, lost it to a Frost Giant during a dice game, traded Freya's hand in marriage to get it back, rescued Freya after the other gods threatened to end him, eaten the apple to hide it from everyone, then given birth to a giant golden aphid or something. And the other gods would've been like, "Well, Loki, we hope you've learned your lesson," and he would've been like, "Oh, yeah, *totally*. Hey, does anyone know where I can find some mistletoe?"

If you're interested in learning more about Loki and centering devotion around him, I highly recommend *Loki and Signy: Lessons on Chaos, Laughter & Loyalty from the Norse Gods* by Lea Svendsen. But for now, let's keep our sights set on the Discordian understanding of Chaos, which will provide a very workable foundation for the practice of Chaos Witchcraft.

Discordian Dance Break
A Quick Note About Loki

Before we go any farther, let's address the fiery half-giant in the room.

A lot of people with an interest in Chaos Witchcraft are going to read this chapter and be like, "Hey, why are we only talking about Eris? What about Loki? After all, he's the god of Chaos. Shouldn't we focus on him? *Why are you subjugating Loki?*"

I promise I've got nothing against Loki. I know he tends to get a bad rap in some Heathen circles, but personally, I think he's great. Plus modern veneration of Loki is at least partially fueled by Tom Hiddleston's portrayal of him in the Marvel Cinematic Universe, and as we've already seen, pop culture occultism is definitely an aspect of Chaos Witchcraft.

But Loki's particular brand of Chaos is not quite what we're exploring here. Eris and Loki do seem to share some traits, but they play very different roles in their respective mythologies. Loki has a consistently strong presence throughout Norse myth, and while he is sometimes depicted as an ally of the Aesir, he is just as often depicted betraying them. In a culture that valued law and structure, Loki represented unpredictable, ominous instability, and knotted twists of fate—things to be respected but warded against.

Eris, on the other hand, was more of an occasional walk-on character in Greek myth. She was certainly seen as trigger-happy, but she generally did not cause problems unless she was specifically provoked, or unless she was instructed to do so by one of the Olympians. But while the machinations of Eris can range from

Elementary, My Good Neikos

The Greek poet and philosopher Empedocles is credited with originating the concept of the Four Elements as objective states of matter: That is, everything in existence can be broken down into the fundamentals of Earth (solid), Air (gas), Fire (plasma/energy), and Water (liquid), which can change, combine, or revert to their original forms based on the effects of two opposing forces, Love (attraction) and Strife (repulsion). Empedocles personified the Elements—which he called roots—as Zeus (Fire), Hades (Air), and Nestis (another name for Persephone; Water), and he referred to Love and Strife as Philotes and Neikos.

And here is another opportunity to practice your paradigm shifting, because according to the *Principia*, the Elements are not Fire, Air, Water, and Earth, or even Zeus, Hades, Hera, and Nestis. For now, you can toss all those Elements right out of your head and change the locks behind them.

Within Discordianism, the Elements are Boom, Pungent, Sweet, Prickle, and Orange.

While ludicrous at first glance, if you look a little deeper, you'll notice that the five Elements line up with the five senses: They represent everything we can hear, smell, taste, touch, and see.

Boom—Audition

Pungent—Olfaction

Sweet—Gustation

Prickle—Somatosensation

Orange—Vision

Metaphorically, this means that by giving birth to the Elements, Eris created everything that can be physically perceived. And if you wanted to be sensible, you could find correspondences between the Discordian Elements and the classical Elements, like so:

Boom—Spirit

Pungent—Air

Sweet—Water

Prickle—Earth

Orange—Fire

But this is Discordianism we're talking about, so sensical isn't going to be the most effective modus operandi. Instead of squeezing the Discordian Elements into a standardized Pagan framework, let them stand independently and evolve into their own unique facets of Chaos Witchcraft. Although the Elemental correspondences are going to come in handy later on, so just tuck them in your back pocket for now.

And speaking of evolution, let's also go back and look at what Hesiod had to say about the two Erises: one likeable, one bloodthirsty. It's that other Eris who stands out in the next phase of Discordian mythology, because Eris has a kid sister. And not a cool, fun one.

Aneris the ... Destructrix? Is That a Word? It Is Now.

Shortly after he gave birth to Eris, Void produced another daughter, whom he named Aneris and whom the *Principia* equates with the Greek goddess Harmonia. Although she was younger than Eris, Aneris quickly grew to be bigger than her sister. And whereas Eris had been born pregnant, Aneris was born sterile, and she was very jealous of her sister's ability to create. And so, whenever Eris brought something into being, Aneris took it away and un-made it, thus becoming the goddess of Non-Being and Destruction. Incidentally, the fact that Aneris stands taller than Eris explains why there are more things that don't exist than things that do.

It turns out that Empedocles was right after all—he just got some of his names wrong. Instead of Philotes, it is Eris as the goddess of Creation who brings the Elements together, and instead of Neikos, it is Aneris who tears them apart.

You might be tempted to say that there is a whole lot of Greek philosophy embedded in Discordianism, and you would not be wrong. But since one of the goals of a Chaos Witch is to be able to switch your beliefs around at will, it's more important to understand that there's a truly ridiculous amount of Discordianism within Greek philosophy.

Crafting with Chaos
Hail, Squat

I was first introduced to Squat the Parking Goddess by a Gardnerian High Priestess after she witnessed my preternatural ability to find good parking in action. "You're favored by Squat!" she exclaimed. And then she added, "But you have to treat her like an important goddess, or else she won't help you find parking spots." I took her advice, going so far as to hang a Sheela-na-gig pendant from my rearview mirror as a votive idol of Squat, and my parking powers have only continued to grow since then.

There is not a lot of information on Squat's origins, other than the unverifiable theory that Discordians "invented" her. Personally, I think she was originally a liminal goddess—like Cardea, the Roman goddess of door hinges—who went on to reinvent herself, but that's just me. Regardless of where she came from, she has become a bona fide modern deity, venerated most often in large metroplexes with limited space for vehicular storage. In *Urban Primitive: Paganism in the Concrete Jungle*, author Raven

Kaldera describes her as "three hundred pounds of warm, round, abundant, billowing flesh," and once invoked, she will find a parking space and fill it with her voluptuousness, saving it for you until you arrive.[13]

As you pull into a parking lot, call upon Squat by reciting the following verse:

> *Squat, Squat,*
> *We like you a lot,*
> *We think you're hot,*
> *Help us find a parking spot.*

If a parking space doesn't reveal itself, try telling her a dirty joke—the oral lore about Squat suggests she's partial to dirty nun jokes, so fire one off. The dirtier the better. If your joke is accepted, you will improbably but immediately find excellent parking.

I unfortunately cannot share my favorite dirty nun joke, which was taught to me by an Episcopal priest, since it is far too filthy to repeat in print. However, the following classic limerick—composed by an anonymous poet—has been offered to Squat on more than one occasion, so it will work for you too.

> *There once was a nun from Siberia,*
> *who was born with a virgin interior,*
> *until a young monk,*
> *jumped into her bunk,*
> *and now she's a mother superior.*

---
13. Kaldera and Schwartzstein, *The Urban Primitive*, 55–57.

Chapter 3
Chaos Explained and Goddesses Snubbed

Of all the occult topics floating about out there, Chaos is probably the most misunderstood. At the same time, it's one of the easiest to comprehend. Accepting Chaos for what it is versus falling back on preconceived notions might be a challenge, but once you do accept it, a whole new realm of possibility will open for you. Literally.

Chaos Condensed

Let's start with a quotation from the *Principia Discordia*: "Magicians, and [their] progeny the scientists, have always taken themselves and their subject in an orderly and sober manner, thereby disregarding an essential metaphysical balance. When Magicians learn to approach philosophy as a malleable art instead of an immutable Truth, and learn to appreciate the absurdity of man's endeavors, then they will be able to pursue their art with a lighter heart, and perhaps gain a clearer understanding of it, and therefore gain more effective magic. CHAOS IS ENERGY."[14]

---

14. Hill and Thornley, *Principia Discordia*, 00061.

Peter J. Carroll elaborated on this concept in *Liber Null & Psychonaut*, defining Chaos as "the 'thing' responsible for the origin and continued action of events." Carroll goes on to say, "It is the force that has caused life to evolve itself out of dust."[15] So that, in a nutshell, is Chaos: It's the primordial Void out of which everything sprang; it's what existed before existence. And it remains the momentum behind all action, and the potential behind all possibilities. And turning those possibilities into probabilities is the ultimate goal of Chaos Witchcraft.

Misconceptions set in, though, when *Chaos* gets used interchangeably with words like *mayhem* or *entropy*. Or, my least favorite, which snuck its way into our cultural lexicon via the rise of role-playing games, *chaotic*.

It's tempting to take in the empirical nature of the Chaos approach to the practice of Witchcraft and think, "This doesn't seem very chaotic." And honestly? It really doesn't. Nor should it. Because from a magical perspective, Chaos is not chaotic. Chaos is something else entirely.

We live in a world that often seems hellbent on sticking to binary thinking, but in Discordian terms, there is only one true binary: Creation and Destruction, which came out of Chaos just as Eris and Aneris came out of Void. Creation and Destruction may occur cyclically, or concurrently, or even simultaneously, but they are two very separate forces. Everything else we would consider opposing binaries is either an illusion or, more commonly, a bimodality.

A bimodality is a fluid polarity: It's basically a gradient scale, with two distinct, apparently opposite plots, but a lot of wiggle room between them. Some things clearly relate to one plot or the other, but some things are similar to both or are only some-

---

15. Carroll, *Liber Null & Psychonaut*, 28.

what similar to one or the other, while other things don't resemble either. Light and dark, for example, aren't really opposites, because both are dynamic—there are points where they are distinct from each other (noon and midnight, say), and points where they are indistinguishable (dusk and dawn). Plus it depends on who's viewing them, and what they're using as a reference point.

Chaos, on the other hand, is not a bimodality, because it has no apparent opposite, nor does it require one. Chaos is not, nor has it ever been, the opposite of Order.

The opposite of Order is Disorder.

Inventing Order

One day, Eris was playing with a pile of things she'd created, and she noticed that when aligned in certain ways, those things created patterns and seemed to make some kind of sense. Eris thought this was great and called her new discovery Order. However, she also noticed that when left in disarray, those same things seemed to not make any sense at all. Eris liked this even better and called this lack of pattern Disorder.

Because Eris was so thrilled with Disorder, she decided to name it Eristic, after herself. And because she and Aneris did not get on well, Eris figured she'd extend an apple branch and declared Order to be Anerisic, after her sister.

What you can take from this parable is that Order and Disorder are artificial constructs, attempts to understand the cosmic powers of Creation and Destruction at the human level. And just like light/dark, big/small, good/bad, positive/negative, or chartreuse/lavender, Order and Disorder are bimodalities. If you took a piece of paper, divided it in half, and wrote Order at the top of one side and Disorder on the top of the other, and started trying to categorize things, you'd realize very quickly that some things are very recognizably one or the other, but some things wouldn't quite be either, and some things would be both.

As a bimodality, Order and Disorder are *apparent*, meaning that they can be perceived, but perceivability makes them *subjective*, reliant on who is looking at them, and how those viewers choose to classify what they see.

Think about it in terms of building a house. There are steps that need to happen chronologically. Those steps can represent Order. However, once construction begins, things are going to get ugly. There's going to be dirt and mud and dust, and unexpected problems are going to arise, and things are going to get off schedule, and there will probably be a few arguments: All of that can represent Disorder. But once construction is complete, we have a house, and that house can once again represent Order. And once the house is lived in for a while, things are going to get cluttered and worn: Disorder.

But at no point in this process are Order and Disorder stationary or objective. Someone might look at the ongoing construction and think, "Wow, this is happening in a very orderly fashion." Whereas someone else might look at the finished house and think, "Geez, none of these design concepts go together. This is very disorderly." And so, Order and Disorder are arbitrary—they are just how we choose to see things, regardless of whether we realize we're making that choice.

My favorite example of the Order/Disorder bimodality comes from the movie *Clueless* (1995), in which the character Amber is described as a Monet—she's pretty at a distance, but up close, she's just a big mess. There's a lot of Disorder going on inside the apparent Order. And while she's not the most likable character, she's not a bad person. And there's more to her personality than just all light or all dark.

Discordian
Dance Break
The Gender of Chaos

You may have noticed that Void is described with male pronouns, and yet he gives birth. This is because gender, like so many things in the universe, is a subjective bimodality.

Page 00050 of the *Principia Discordia* states, "Disorder is simply unrelated information viewed through some particular grid. But, like 'relation', no-relation is a concept. Male, like female, is an idea about sex. To say that male-ness is 'absence of female-ness', or vice versa, is a matter of definition and metaphysically arbitrary."[16]

There are many, many people in the world who are perfectly content with the gender they were assigned at birth, to the point where they may not ever give it more than a passing thought, and that's great! There is absolutely nothing wrong with that. But individually, your gender expression is something over which you have complete control. Regardless of societal norms, *you* have the final say over what you wear, how you style yourself, and what mannerisms you project.

Allowing yourself to be aware of what you're capable of changing, even if you choose not to change anything, is an act of claiming power.

Also, this is a metaphor. Just keep that in mind.

16. Hill and Thornley, *Principia Discordia*, 00050.

Surfing the Grids

Here's what we know about Order and Disorder so far. They are:

Artificial.

Bimodal.

Apparent.

Subjective.

But on top of all that, Order and Disorder are *cultural*.

The *Principia Discordia* defines culture as a group of people who look at the world through a particular grid, a grid being a given belief system, philosophy, or religion.[17] When Chaos Witches paradigm shift, we're actively choosing which grid we want to look through. Some grids make things look Orderly, which means those grids are exhibiting what's known as the Aneristic Principle. Other grids make things appear Disorderly, which means those grids are exhibiting what's known as the Eristic Principle.

What's important to remember here is that those principles are in the grids, not in the world. For example, my eyeglasses have blue-tinted lenses, so when I wear them, everything around me takes on a blue tinge. But that tinge is in the lenses, not in whatever I happen to be viewing. Likewise, if I put on someone else's glasses, everything would look wonky, and if I tried to navigate my surroundings while wearing them, I would probably fall more than I already do. But that wonkiness is also in the lenses, not in my immediate environment.

Some cultures look at apparent Order and assume that it is somehow fundamentally correct, which leads them to believe that Disorder is incorrect—think about how some sects of Fun-

---
17. Hill and Thornley, *Principia Discordia*, 00050.

damentalist Christianity aver that anything they don't approve of is satanic. This is called the Aneristic Illusion. Other cultures look at apparent Disorder and decide that *it* is somehow fundamentally correct, thereby concluding that Disorder is the natural way of things, and that Order is unnatural—like an armchair revolutionary who doesn't understand the difference between anarchism and anarchy. This is called the Eristic Illusion. And these are illusions, because they are entirely in our heads—they are what we choose to believe, whether or not we realize we're making that choice.

And because Order and Disorder are bimodal, they exist on spectrums, governed by the one true binary of Creation and Destruction. Order can be Creative and result in structurally sound designs, or it can be Destructive and result in systemic oppression. Disorder can be Creative, which is the inspiration behind a lot of really cool art. But it can also be Destructive, such as when sports fans riot and set cars on fire after their favorite team wins a big game.

Something to keep in mind here is that apparent Order and Disorder are not respectively good and bad, or vice versa. But just as every action has an equal and opposite reaction, so too does the haphazard application of Order and Disorder have consequences... as we can see in the following myth, which is foundational to Discordianism.

The Original Snub

Picture it: Mount Olympus, thirty-two hundred years ago (give or take). All the gods had gathered to celebrate the wedding of the sea goddess Thetis and the mortal hero Peleus—all of them, that is, except Eris, who had a reputation as a troublemaker and therefore wasn't invited.

The festivities were in full swing, and everyone was having a *marvelous* time, when suddenly, the doors to the banquet hall flew open, and Eris cartwheeled in, flipping through the air and landing in a dramatic, action movie pose. With all trepidatious eyes upon her, she drew back and lobbed a golden apple into the middle of the dance floor, then twerked backward out of the room before anyone could stop her, and, according to Discordian lore, went off to enjoy a hotdog.

Engraved into the apple was Τι Καλλίστη (For the Fairest), and immediately, five goddesses dove for it, among them Hera, Athena, and Aphrodite. (The other two were never identified, but I like to assume they were Artemis and Persephone.) Things got very tense, very quickly; strongly worded critiques were thrown. And, to regain control of the situation, Zeus announced a beauty pageant, the winner of which would receive the golden apple.

The goddesses agreed to the terms, and Zeus dispatched Hermes to find a judge. Hermes settled on Paris of Troy, a part-time shepherd and full-time nepo baby, who had a reputation for objectivity and could allegedly be counted on to make an unbiased decision. Immediately, the goddesses tried to bribe him: Hera offered him sovereignty, Athena offered him military might, and Aphrodite offered him the love of the most beautiful woman in the world.

"Sold," yelled Paris. And he presented the apple to Aphrodite. (So much for objectivity.)

At the time, the title of Most Beautiful Woman in the World belonged to an ingenue named Helen, who was inopportunely married to Menelaus, the king of Sparta. Regardless, she and Paris had a meet-cute and ran off together. A *profoundly* unamused Menelaus pursued them, and the subsequent series of events eventually led to the Trojan War.

So that's the myth as it's commonly understood. But as is so often the case with mythology, there is a whole lot more to the story. Let's deconstruct it.

First of all, the marriage was not consensual.

There was a prophecy (standard issue in those days) that if Thetis had a child with another god, that child would grow up to overthrow Zeus. Zeus did not like this one bit, and so he decided to marry Thetis off to the mortal Peleus, thus circumventing the prophecy entirely. Peleus, having no idea how to woo a goddess, went to the river god Proteus for advice, who explained that Thetis was a shape-shifter: All Peleus had to do was sneak up on her, tackle her, and hold on for dear life as she assumed different forms. Eventually, she'd tucker out and agree to marry him.

This inexplicably worked, probably because these myths were originally written down by the ancient Greek equivalent of tech bros. Thetis and Peleus ended up engaged, and the prophecy was averted, but Zeus knew he'd dealt in some shadiness to make that happen. Zeus not inviting Eris to the wedding is basically a refusal to accept that there could be consequences to his actions—in his mind, if he (literally) didn't invite trouble, there wouldn't be any trouble. Except...

The apple should have gone to Thetis.

It's straight out of Etiquette 101—if you're at a wedding, and someone hands you *anything* marked For the Fairest, just give it to the bride and go on with your life. I shouldn't even have to explain this, *Hera.*

Oh, and by the way, there was another prophecy that everyone conveniently forgot about.

While pregnant, Paris's mother had a portentous dream that her son would be responsible for the fall of Troy, so once Paris was born, she and her husband passed him off to a local shepherd and were like, "Handle this problem for us." The shepherd was ultimately unwilling to unalive an innocent baby, so Paris grew to adulthood and returned to his parents, who rationalized that prophecies maybe weren't that big of a deal after all.

And then Paris eloped with Helen, and Troy got paved over by the Spartans. Go figure.

But here's the weird thing. Hermes is the god of divination: As such, he would have been fully aware of the prophecy haunting Paris. So why would he pick Paris as a judge, even though that decision would make a whole lot of carnage inevitable?

Was Hermes secretly working for Eris?

Spoiler alert: He totally was. And I am going to table that for now, but I promise we'll get back to it soon.

That Escalated Quickly

From a Discordian standpoint, Zeus's actions in the myth of the Original Snub reflect Destructive Order: He was attempting to restrict individual liberties and get everyone to do what he wanted so that he could remain in charge. Thetis, on the other hand, represents Creative Disorder—her power to change shape is indicative of free and unfettered expression.

By arranging her marriage to Peleus and by Peleus physically restraining her, Destructive Order was imposed on Creative Disorder. And whenever Destructive Order is imposed on Creative Disorder, mythologically or otherwise, Destructive Disorder results. This is known as the Law of Eristic Escalation. To sum up:

Zeus, Peleus, Menelaus, and Paris's Parents = Destructive Order

Thetis, Eris, Hermes, and Assorted Shepherds = Creative Disorder

Everything That Happened After the Apple Hit the Dance Floor = Destructive Disorder

As a Chaos Witch, this is what you will use in place of more debatable occult guidelines like the Threefold Law, which I will investigate at length in the chapter on Chaos Ethics, so stay tuned.

Putting the Chaos in Chaos

I mentioned in chapter 1 that Austin Osman Spare referred to the shared consciousness of the universe as Kia, and I will add here that Peter J. Carroll described Kia as life force, in which Chaos is concentrated to spark human consciousness. Carroll also theorized that between Chaos and the physical world, and between Kia and waking thought, there is a sort of non-substance called Aether, which is basically all the possibilities that Chaos has generated, but which have not yet (and may or may not ever) come to fruition.[18]

By working within this unfamiliar but accommodating paradigm, focusing thoughts on specific desires or statements of intent, and manipulating matter in certain ways—say, lighting candles, burning incense, or drawing sigils—bits of Aether can be coerced into solidification, which in turn can result in controlled coincidences. This is the basis of Chaos Magic.

To put it all in Discordian terms: Out of Chaos come Eris and Aneris, and out of Eris come the five Elements (Aether). By practicing Witchcraft, and by Ordering and Disordering things in innovative ways, the intangible concepts of Boom, Pungent, Sweet, Prickle, and Orange can have concrete, substantial effects.

A lot of people hear the term *Chaos Magic* and assume it's something vaguely sinister, or at the very least disorganized, but

---
18. Carroll, *Liber Null & Psychonaut*, 28–29.

in reality, *chaos* is an adjective that means "action-based." Just as Chaos itself is the force behind activity, Chaos Magic—and, by extension, Chaos Witchcraft—is an active, experimental approach to magical practice, with an emphasis on achieving verifiable and repeatable results.

All that said, I do comprehend that *chaotic* is going to mean ... well, *chaotic*, no matter how much I kind of wish it didn't. But for those of us who are Witches, Magicians, Sorcerers, Cunningfolk, Tasseomancers, or what have you, it's important that we fully understand the words we use to describe our practices, so that we can direct our wills as accurately as possible to get the results we want.

Crafting with Chaos
Rolling for Ism

I honestly do not remember where I first came across the following apparatus, although I want to say Peter J. Carroll originally developed it, so I'm just going to attribute it to him. Regardless, as a method for gaining practical experience in moving back and forth between different belief systems, it cannot be beat.

Obtain a six-sided die, and assign a different theism to each number, like so:

1. Atheism
2. Duotheism
3. Henotheism
4. Monotheism
5. Pantheism
6. Polytheism

Role the die and look at the number. Whatever theism comes up is your new religious belief system.

For instance, in trying this technique out for myself, I rolled my die and got the number four: monotheism. My goal, then, was to restructure my current beliefs into a monotheistic worldview, like so:

Discordianism is a monotheistic religion based entirely on the worship of Eris, the goddess of discord. We have myths that come out of ancient Greek religion that talk about Eris interacting with other gods and goddesses, but those are just stories used to teach, and to give us a better understanding of Eris herself. There are tales of Eris in conflict with other goddesses, but again, these are just stories. Eris is both Creation and Destruction: We have no need of any other goddesses, since Eris is more than capable of handling both. And while it would be easy to say, "Oh, other goddesses are just aspects of Eris..." No. There aren't any other goddesses. There really is just Eris. And this is what I fully believed for twenty-four hours.

Role your die every morning for five days, and every day, rework your core beliefs to fit your new theism. You may discover that some theisms are more comfortable than others, or you may be surprised to learn that your beliefs adapt well to all of them. Either way, you will find it easier and easier to shift your beliefs around as needed, which is a huge step toward using those beliefs as magical tools.

Chapter 4

Discordian Seasons and Apostles of Eris

It may feel counterintuitive to think of organized religion as doing anything positive in the world, especially for those of us who are actively attempting to deconstruct or distance ourselves from it. But we have to remember that most religions didn't pop into existence in their current capitalistic forms. As Paul Huson put it in his iconic book *Mastering Witchcraft*, "Ironically, you will find that all the innovators and founders of religions were revolutionaries in their time who took issue with their parent religions and were usually labeled heretics of one sort or another for their pains."[19]

Most religions start off, if not entirely beneficial, then at least diverting—something to give adherents a respite from the toils of daily living. It isn't until someone gets into a position of authority and thinks, "You know, I'll bet I could make a decent living if I bottled and sold this..." that problems metastasize.

But this is where Discordianism comes in handy. It can assist you in sifting through all the crud that has accumulated around religions and dig out the useful core tenets. Plus, you don't have to wrestle

---
19. Huson, *Mastering Witchcraft*, 19–20.

with it all by yourself. As a Chaos Witch, you have access to the Apostles of Eris, who can guide you along your way through the seasons they represent.

Seasons of Philotes

The Discordian calendar is the same length as the standard Gregorian calendar, although it is divided into five seasons, each of which is made up of seventy-three days, organized into five-day weeks. These seasons are, in chronological order:

Chaos (January 1 to March 14)

Discord (March 15 to May 26)

Confusion (May 27 to August 7)

Bureaucracy (August 8 to October 19)

Aftermath (October 20 to December 31)

At first glance, the names of the seasons may strike you as ominous. But just as Chaos in a magical sense is neither good nor bad, so are the seasons themselves neutral in their overall meanings. The Season of Chaos is about beginnings; Discord is a shift in balance; Confusion is a change in perception; Bureaucracy is structure; and Aftermath represents both endings and looking ahead.

Think about it like this. A baby is born, moving from the safety and comfort of the womb into a bright, loud, overwhelming environment (Chaos). The baby is initially unaware of their own sentience, but eventually, they learn the two words every parent dreads—*no* and *why*—and they begin schooling, where, for the first, jarring time, they must interact with people outside of their immediate family unit (Discord).

Discordian Seasons and Apostles of Eris

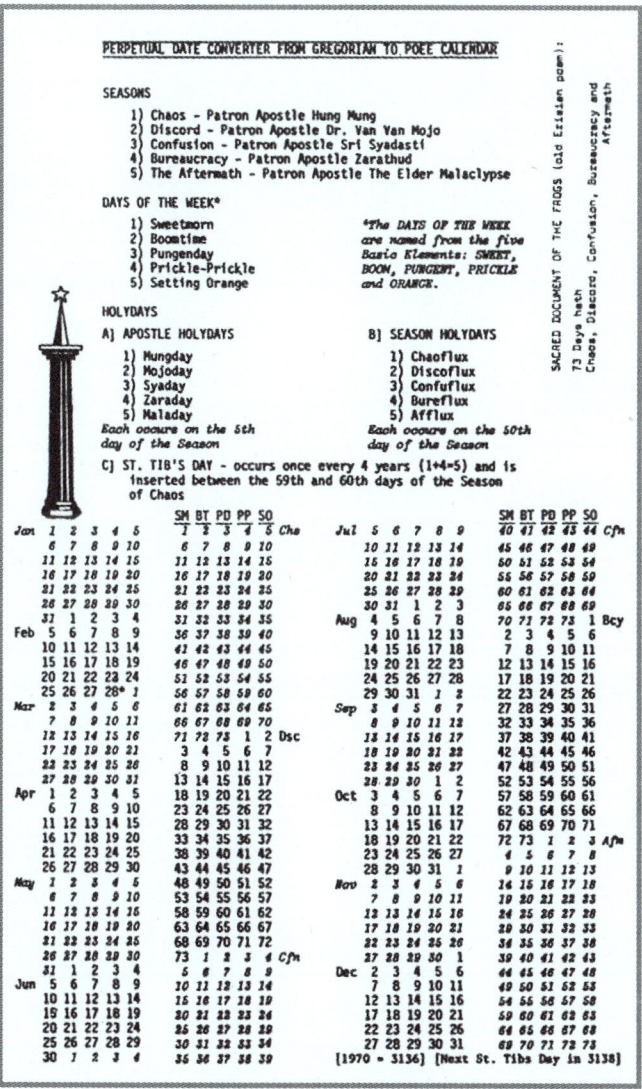

Discordian Calendar

Things move along relatively smoothly for a while, but suddenly, puberty hits, and their body starts changing in disconcerting and unexpected ways; their education changes as well, and they become dimly aware that the world is a lot more complicated and nuanced than they may have been led to believe (Confusion).

Eventually, it's time to strike out on their own and become an actual grownup, which means finding sources of income, and figuring out how to navigate the labyrinths of insurance, taxes, and human resources (Bureaucracy). They may also end up starting a family of their own, parenthood being about as bureaucratic as you can get: As Deborah Lipp once wrote in a blog post, "Mothers need management skills. There's like, paperwork."[20] And as they begin to move into their twilight years, they will reflect on their life experiences and start preparing for the next stage of existence, be that reincarnation or a *really* long nap, depending on their belief system (Aftermath).

The Discordian calendar can be a challenge to work with at first, but it's another great exercise in paradigm shifting. The more you actively engage with it—like, say, celebrating Samhain on Aftermath 12 instead of October 31—the more comfortable you'll become with it. Remember that paradigm shifting is a skill like any other: It takes practice, but sooner than later, it will become second nature.

---

20. Lipp, "Thoughts on Motherhood."

Discordian Dance Break

Katsaridaphobia

Page 00027 of the *Principia Discordia* features a small sketch of a cockroach, flanked by a handwritten caption: "'This is St. Gulik. He is the Messenger of the Goddess. A different age from ours called him Hermes. Many people called him by many names. He is a Roach."

His full title is St. Gulik the Stoned, and the fact that he's a roach is a terrible, terrible pun. As it also says in the *Principia*, "There is historic disagreement concerning whether [the Apple of Discord] was of metallic gold or Acapulco." In other words, if you smoke a roach, you'll receive messages from the Goddess. It probably goes without saying, but Mal-2 and Lord Omar were both big fans of the Devil's Lettuce, and the sheer number of marijuana jokes in the *Principia* reflects that.

But here's where things get interesting: Remember how, in the myth of the Original Snub, Hermes managed to pick the one judge whose actions would result in the most devastating consequences? If St. Gulik is the messenger of the Goddess, then Hermes was (and still is) the wingman of Eris, and *how freaking cool is that*?

Modern Discordian lore suggests that if you see a roach, you should a) accept it as a message from Eris, and b) squash it to let Eris know the message was received. Since I live in South Texas, I get a *lot* of messages from Eris, of the gargantuan, flying variety. Don't get me wrong: I am flattered that she wants to reach out. But whenever I turn on my kitchen light, and one of her messages lunges out of the shadows before gleefully skittering under the refrigerator, I do sometimes wish I'd stayed Episcopalian.

Incidentally, page 00040 of the Principia states that "Sri Syadasti should not be confused with Blessed St. Gulik the Stoned, who is not the same person but is the same Apostle." If you run into any challenges connecting with Sri Syadasti, try touching base with Hermes instead.

Five Holy Helpers

According to the *Principia Discordia*, the Apostles of Eris are the pioneers of Discordianism. But as literary devices, the Apostles are personifications of major world religions and ideologies—Taoism, African Diasporic religions, Hinduism, classical Greek philosophy, and the Abrahamic faiths—all of which have, in one way or another, subversively promoted the advancement of Creative Disorder. Each of the Apostles has governance over one of the seasons, and each of them made a significant contribution to Discordianism. In order of appearance, the Apostles are:

Hung Mung, Patron of Chaos

Dr. Van Van Mojo, Patron of Discord

Sri Syadasti, Patron of Confusion

Zarathud, Patron of Bureaucracy

The Elder Malaclypse, Patron of Aftermath

In *Oven-Ready Chaos*, Phil Hine presents a short Discordian Opening Ritual, composed by a Discordian known only as Prince Prance.[21] By breaking this rite into five parts, we're left with a (mildly edited) prayer for each of the Apostles, which you can use as petitions whenever you're exploring the belief systems they represent.

---

21. Hine, *Oven-Ready Chaos*, 26–27.

Hung Mung

Hung Mung (more accurately transliterated as Hong Meng) is the patron saint of the Season of Chaos and the personification of Daoism. Unlike the other Apostles, Hung Mung existed in pre-Discordian mythology: He was first mentioned in the ancient Chinese *Zhuangzi*—one of the foundational texts of Daoism—as a primordial being, akin to Khaos or Void. Additionally, his name is a play on words, translating to "Mists of Chaos," "Vast Obscurity," or (I promise I am not making this up) "Big Goose Dummy."

As a philosophy, Daoism espouses compassion, detachment, humility, moderation, and spontaneity, and Daoists work to align themselves with the Dao, or the natural order of things. If you want to weave any of these concepts into your Chaos Witchcraft, pray to Hung Mung before you begin.

The Sacred Chao

Hung Mung's contribution to Discordianism is the Sacred Chao, the symbol featured on the scroll shown to Mal-2 and Lord Omar by that talking chimpanzee. The section of the Chao with the pentagon is called the Hodge, which represents the Aneristic Principle; likewise, the section of the Chao with the apple is called the Podge, which represents the Eristic Principle.

According to the *Principia*, the Sacred Chao "symbolizes absolutely everything anyone need ever know about absolutely anything, and more! It even symbolizes everything not worth knowing, depicted by the empty space surrounding the Hodge-Podge."[22] In layman's terms, what's "worth knowing" is the true nature of Order and Disorder—they are perceptions of Chaos, not Chaos itself. (The Sacred Chao has also become a ubiquitous symbol of Discordianism, and wearing a Sacred Chao pendant or accessory is a good way to let other Chaotes out in the wild know that you, too, are part of the Greatest Show on Earth.)

The Prince Prance Prayer to Hung Mung

Blessed Apostle Hung Mung, Great Sage of Cathay,
Balance the Hodge and Podge and grant me equilibrium.

Dr. Van Van Mojo

Dr. Van Van Mojo is the patron saint of the Season of Discord and the personification of African Traditional Religions (ATRs), sometimes referred to as African Diasporic Religions. If you are an initiate of a particular ATR, or if you are part of a culture in which a given ATR is prevalent, Dr. Mojo can act as a bridge between your background and your Chaos practice. If you are not part of one of these cultures, Dr. Mojo can still help you draw respectful inspiration from them without falling into appropriation.

For instance, Catholic iconography is often utilized in ATRs to represent spirits and divinities. This is a form of assimilation, which

---

22. Hill and Thornley, *Principia Discordia*, 00049.

occurs whenever a marginalized group adopts the traditions of a dominant group, either to survive or because the dominant group has imposed those traditions on the marginalized group. If you need to hide your Witchcraft in plain sight or disguise it within the trappings of a mainstream faith, Dr. Mojo can offer direction.

Within Discordianism, Dr. Mojo is revered for creating the Turkey Curse, a powerful, magical act of Creative Disorder, and you'll learn how to throw the Turkey Curse later in this book. Incidentally, according to the *Principia*, the POEE and the Erisian Liberation Front are at odds over the identity of the Patron of Discord: The POEE asserts that it's Dr. Van Van Mojo, but the Erisian Liberation Front claims the true Apostle is named Patamunzo Lingananda.[23]

Basically, Discordians honor the Patron of Discord by arguing over who the Patron of Discord is, which is decidedly on brand.

The Prince Prance Prayer to Dr. Van Van Mojo

Blessed Apostle Van Van Mojo, Doctor of Hoodoo and Vexes,
Give me the Voodoo Power and confuse my enemies.

Sri Syadasti

Sri Syadasti is the patron saint of the Season of Confusion and the personification of Dharmic religions like Hinduism, Jainism, Sikhism, and Buddhism. These religions emphasize the importance of meditation, and a common thread between them is belief in reincarnation as determined by Karma, or the sum of one's actions—good and bad—in one's current and previous lives. Additionally, Dharmic religions are pluralistic, in that they acknowledge the existence of more than one path to enlightenment and embrace diversity in both

---

23. Hill and Thornley, *Principia Discordia*, 00039.

personal opinion and representation of the Divine. If you're trying to get your brain around meditation, or even if you're having trouble finding suitable votive images of the gods you venerate, Sri Syadasti is your go-to guy.

Sri Syadasti's contribution to Discordianism is his name, which can be used as a contemplative mantra. His full name (allegedly Sanskrit), in its entirety, is Sri Syadasti Syadavaktavya Syadasti Syannasti Syadasti Cavaktavyasca Syadasti Syannasti Syadavatavyasca Syadasti Syannasti Syadavaktavyasca, which (again allegedly) translates to "All Affirmations Are True in Some Sense, False in Some Sense, Meaningless in Some Sense, True and False in Some Sense, True and Meaningless in Some Sense, False and Meaningless in Some Sense, and True and False and Meaningless in Some Sense."[24]

If you decide to experiment with his full name in meditation, feel free to stick with the English translation, rather than trying to memorize the Sanskrit version. I promise he won't mind.

The Prince Prance Prayer to Sri Syadasti

> *Blessed Apostle Sri Syadasti, Patron of Psychedelia,*
> *Teach me the relative truth and blow my mind.*

Zarathud

Zarathud, also known as Zarathud the Staunch and Zarathud the Incorrigible, is the patron saint of the Season of Bureaucracy and the personification of classical Greek philosophy. He is also the personification of ceremonial magic, because if there's *anything* out there that epitomizes bureaucracy, it's ceremonial magic.

The *Principia* explains that Zarathud was once a priest but became a hermit after getting himself labeled an Offender of the

---

[24]. Hill and Thornley, *Principia Discordia*, 00039–00040.

Faith.[25] We're not told what he did to earn that designation, but he can definitely act as a mentor if you're studying philosophy, curious about Goetic ritual, or just stubbornly engaging in any activity that would get you burned at the stake in Medieval Europe.

Zarathud's contribution to Discordianism is the Pentabarf, also known as the Five Commandments, the "rules" to which all Discordians must adhere. A full explanation of the Pentabarf can be found in chapter 9.

The Prince Prance Prayer to Zarathud

> *Blessed Apostle Zarathud, Hard-Nosed Hermit,*
> *Grant me the Erisian doubt, and the constancy of Chaos.*

The Elder Malaclypse

The Elder Malaclypse is the patron saint of the Season of Aftermath and the personification of Abrahamic religions—Judaism, Christianity, and Islam. The *Principia* describes him as a wandering wise man who followed a five-pointed star across Ancient Mediterrania.[26] Despite his associations, he's a lot less Southern Baptist Convention, and a lot more Jesus Chasing the Moneylenders Out of the Temple.

The Elder Malaclypse appears as a character in *The Illuminatus! Trilogy*, where he is depicted as an immortal, shape-shifting being of pure intuition, impersonating Billy Graham, Satan, Jean-Paul Sartre, and a cabdriver. He also masqueraded as Jesus after the crucifixion, pretty much just because he could, and he likes to amuse himself by inventing conspiracy theories.

---

25. Hill and Thornley, *Principia Discordia*, 00040.
26. Hill and Thornley, *Principia Discordia*, 00040.

Prayers to Malaclypse are appropriate if you're trying to incorporate a particular Abrahamic technique into your practice, or if you have no palpable sense of self-preservation and want to go on an adventure.

The Elder Malaclypse's contribution to Discordianism is his role as the namesake of Malaclypse the Younger, which is actually a pretty big deal—after all, if Malaclypse the Younger hadn't had someone to name himself after, we might not have Discordianism today.

Portrait of the Author as the Elder Malaclypse,
Courtesy of Lucas E. Wagner

The bigger point here being that it's customary within many Pagan and Witchcraft traditions to take on a new name, and Discordianism is no different. As it says in the *Principia*: "Discordians have a tradition of assuming HOLY NAMES. This is not unique with Erisianism, of course. I suppose that Pope Paul is the son of Mr. and Mrs. VI? And also TITLES OF MYSTICAL IMPORT."[27]

If you're thinking about adopting a magical name as part of your Chaos Witchcraft journey, you absolutely have my blessing. Even my dad calls me Thumper at this point, but it is surprisingly not the name on my birth certificate. And if you're having trouble settling on a new name, the Elder Malaclypse can guide you to the right one.

The Prince Prance Prayer to the Elder Malaclypse
> *Blessed Apostle Malaclypse, Elder Saint of Discordia,*
> *Grant me illumination and protect me from stupidity.*

Crafting with Chaos
The Five-Sided Circle

Witches cast circles for a variety of reasons: to delineate sacred space, for protection, or to mark the beginning of a ritual. All these are perfectly valid, but from a psychological perspective, casting a circle draws your attention inward, directing your focus toward the magical or meditative work you're doing and away from outside distractions.

Circle casting can be an elaborate affair, but it does not have to be. All you really need is a quiet space where you won't be interrupted, with enough room to stand and turn around. You'll also need to know the cardinal directions of the area—use a compass if you're not sure.

Stand in the center of your space and clap five times, slowly and deliberately. Then raise your arms to the east,

---
27. Hill and Thornley, *Principia Discordia*, 00035.

hands out and fingers splayed, and chant: *Hung Mung, Hung Mung, Hung Mung, Hung Mung, Hung Mung.*

Jump as if startled by a loud noise. Then, with your arms still out and fingers still splayed, turn to the south and chant: *Van Van Mojo, Van Van Mojo, Van Van Mojo, Van Van Mojo, Van Van Mojo.*

Crinkle your nose, as if it's suddenly been hit with an acrid aroma. Turn to the west and chant: *Sri Syadasti, Sri Syadasti, Sri Syadasti, Sri Syadasti, Sri Syadasti.*

Lick your lips, as if they're coated in your favorite flavor of lip balm. Then turn to the north and chant: *Zarathud, Zarathud, Zarathud, Zarathud, Zarathud.*

Shake your hands, as if they've fallen asleep, and you're trying to get rid of the pins and needles. Then point your left hand toward the ceiling and your right hand toward the ground, and chant: *Malaclypse, Malaclypse, Malaclypse, Malaclypse, Malaclypse.*

Blink rapidly, as if you're trying to get spots out of your eyes.

Once your ritual or meditation is complete, you can dismiss the Apostles thusly:

Face the east, raise your arms in salute, and shout (or whisper with intent, if you've got roommates): *Thank you for hearing this rite, Hung Mung! So long!*

Turn to the south and shout: *Thank you for censing this rite, Van Van Mojo! Farewell!*

Turn to the west and shout: *Thank you for spicing this rite, Sri Syadasti! Auf Wiedersehen!*

Turn to the north and shout: *Thank you for stoking this rite, Zarathud! Good night!*

Point your right hand to the ceiling and your left hand toward the ground and shout: *Thank you for watching this rite, Malaclypse! The sun has gone to bed and so must I!*

Once the circle is closed, you can go about the rest of your day or evening, secure in the knowledge that the Discordian Apostles are aware of your existence and grateful for your attention.

Chapter 5
Principles of Chaos Witchcraft

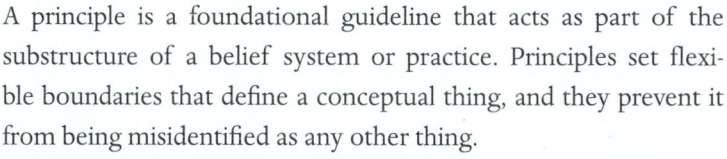

A principle is a foundational guideline that acts as part of the substructure of a belief system or practice. Principles set flexible boundaries that define a conceptual thing, and they prevent it from being misidentified as any other thing.

Within the realm of Chaos Witchcraft, it is tempting to write off principles as nonessential, especially since the "whatever we want it to be" mentality is still so pervasive in contemporary occultism. But even Discordianism, for all its inherent insanity, has principles in place to differentiate itself from other belief systems. Principles help explain what a given magical practice is and is not, which in turn will help you approach and apply it efficiently.

Hine Sight Is 20/20

In *Condensed Chaos*, Phil Hine offers six principles of Chaos Magic. They are as follows, in the order he presents them (although he makes it clear that they are not set in stone and can be rearranged, emphasized, or discarded as necessary):

Avoidance of Dogma

Personal Experience

Technical Excellence

Deconditioning

Diverse Approaches

Gnosis

To Hine's list of principles, I'm going to add two more:

Immersion

Discipline

Let's consider them individually and see how they are applicable to the work of the Chaos Witch.

Avoidance of Dogma

Chaos Witchcraft does not come with a set of built-in beliefs, nor is there a specific Higher Power overseeing Chaos Witchcraft who dictates what we may or may not do (not even Eris). Beliefs are subjective, and we can change our minds regarding what we believe whenever we need to. There is no right way to practice Chaos Witchcraft, and the big-time unexpected benefit of this is that it is okay to be wrong—anytime we're wrong about something, we can learn from it and shift our beliefs accordingly.

Personal Experience

This is the "doing" aspect of Chaos Witchcraft. Remember how I mentioned that Chaos Magic is results driven? We get those results by actively practicing and experimenting with magic. Instead of just reading what other people (including me) have done and accepting it at face value, try things out, bend a few set "rules," and find out what works for you.

Incidentally, another part of personal experience is documentation: That is, writing down all the things we're doing. On one hand, this is so that we can track the results we're getting, but it's also so that we can have a record of the routes we took to get to those results (and so that we don't overlook any variables along the way). If you want to practice Chaos Witchcraft, invest in journals; this is my sage advice to you.

Technical Excellence

Maybe it's because I'm a Virgo, or because I have OCD, or because I'm a Virgo with OCD, but if I can't do something perfectly on the first try, then I don't want to do it at all. And this is something I've really had to struggle with throughout my occult career, because magic relies on both talent and skill, and skill takes time to develop.

None of us are going to be Grand High Chaos Witches right out of the gate. But what we can do is figure out where our talents and interests lie, focus our efforts there, document the outcomes of the work we do (see earlier), and then start over and try again until we achieve the results we're looking for. And then do it again and again until we get those results consistently.

Deconditioning

This is the principle that most deserves its own chapter, but for the moment, I'll just say this: Deconditioning is the process of becoming less attached to ingrained attitudes and beliefs, so that we can view the world around us more objectively. Our dominant society is based on Protestant-Christian ethics, and whether we're aware of it or not, those ethics have a massive influence on us. In the United States, we allegedly have separation of Church and State, yet the only religious observance recognized as a federal holiday is a Christian one (Christmas Day). If we're going to practice effective Chaos Witchcraft, we've got to learn how to disengage from that conditioning.

Diverse Approaches

We've already determined that there is no one right way to practice Chaos Witchcraft, and since our beliefs are (ideally) malleable, we shouldn't be afraid to think outside of the box—or just burn the box down—and explore different techniques and systems to see which ones bring us the payoffs we're after. The downside is that this can quickly lead into some sticky territory between cultural appropriation and open/closed practices, which I'll cover in chapter 9.

Gnosis

Gnosis is the easiest principle to explain, but the toughest to put into practice. Long story short, in the context of Chaos Witchcraft, gnosis is the altered state of consciousness necessary to work magic. If paradigm shifting is choosing which grid we look through, gnosis is changing the angle through which the grid is viewed.

We actually slip into gnosis all the time without realizing it—my personal favorite permutation being highway hypnosis—but the trick is being able to reach gnosis on command, versus accidentally. There are people in this world who can snap their fingers, and *bam*, ritual trance, ready to go. I am not one of those people. Instead, I rely on what are called inhibitory (passive) and excitatory (active) exercises to get there.

Inhibitory exercises are used to calm the mind and facilitate a meditative state. Deep breathing, for instance, is inhibitory, as is staring into a candle flame for an extended length of time. Excitatory exercises, by comparison, get the blood flowing. Think of how ecstatic it feels to attend a concert, as you and the rest of the audience dance and sing along with the performers. A runner's high—the euphoria experienced by some athletes during or immediately following strenuous activity—is another example of an excitatory state.

You know how, in every documentary about cults, they bring in a deprogrammer to talk about brainwashing? All those techniques—chanting, sleep deprivation, diet restriction, etc.—are examples of things we can use as inhibitory and/or excitatory pathways to gnosis. Although maybe try them out on your own, or with a friend who has healthy boundaries. Please don't join a cult. That would be bad.

Immersion

This is the first of my own additions to the Chaos principles list. Whatever it is you're studying as part of your Witchcraft practice, you should be willing to go all in. There's a misconception out there that Chaos Witchcraft relies on laziness and half-hearted efforts, when in fact, the exact opposite is true: Chaotes will commit to their transient beliefs like nobody's business.

Let's look at it this way: Say I want to create my own Witchcraft Tradition. I work out the basics, do some research and figure out how to cast a circle, assemble some tools, pull some rituals out of various books, dedicate myself to a goddess, and cobble it all together into a regular practice that works well for me. This is an Eclectic approach.

If I do all these steps, then convert to Islam for six months so that I can get a better grip on *salat* (that is, requisite prayer five times a day), then bid Allah *ma'a as-salama* and switch back to Paganism to incorporate my experiences into my personal Witchcraft practice, *that's* a Chaos approach.

Discipline

This is the second of my amendments, which could also be called doggedness or determination. The gist is that if I were trying to come up with a new method of spellcasting, I would keep working at the technique until I've gotten the results I'm looking for, ignoring adversity and not giving up until the work is completed. And then I would begin again and repeat the process to confirm that those results are consistent.

But discipline also means keeping a healthy balance alive in my practice: juxtaposing between mirth and reverence; getting a kick out of what I'm doing while taking it seriously; finding sacredness in the impertinent and using that as a source of power; reminding myself that nothing is true and everything is permitted, especially in moments when my rational mind is stomping its feet and shrieking, "No. Only one way. Must do things that way."

There is no one way, especially when it comes to Chaos Witchcraft. But it's still a specific thing with its own parameters. And once you're able to perceive them and work within them efficiently, you can Molotov cocktail those restrictions and build something abominable and transcendent out of the ashes. And then do it all over again to prove that it works. And that, I think, is when no one will be able to argue you're not practicing Chaos Witchcraft.

Not even yours truly. And I'm pretty excited about that too.

Lust of Result

Since you've been learning about principles, now is a good time to bring up a topic more precautionary in nature. While not a principle in and of itself, it is something worth keeping in mind as you navigate Chaos Witchcraft.

Lust of result is exactly what it sounds like: being so emotionally invested in the outcome of a magical working that the working itself is negated.

It does seem contradictory—after all, shouldn't you want your spells to work? Of course you should! But if you get tangled up in fantasizing about what you're going to do if-and-when-and-if a given spell achieves its purpose, or if you start worrying about whether or not you did enough to manifest your goals, you're decreasing the probability of achieving them.

Sometimes, when I have a particular spell in mind, I research and cross-reference and dig up herbal correspondences and planetary associations and swipe incantations out of old grimoires and rewrite them for the task at hand and fixate on incense blends and generally just let my hyperfocus run wild. However, once the spell is cast, and once the candles melt away or the burnt offerings set off the smoke detector, I set everything aside and move on, letting the magic work without any further interference on my part. And it was a challenge to learn how to do that, but it was vital if I was going to progress as a Witch.

When you cast a spell, you need to do so with utmost confidence (*not* cockiness, mind you; just confidence), and lust of result gets in the way of that. It's a lot like shooting a gun—I can stress over my ability to use the gun correctly, and let my anxiety get the better of me, and get so worked up that I become a danger to myself and others. Or, I can take a deep breath, clear my head, aim, and pull the trigger, which will dramatically increase my chance of hitting my target.

Having been to a gun range before, I can say that my first couple of shots were like, "*Aaaaaahhh*, I am wielding a loaded weapon, and I am uncomfortable." But once I settled down and focused, I was able to zero in on what I was doing; my aim improved, and

I got sort of good at it. And it's honestly the same with Witchcraft. It just takes patience and practice.

Sometimes, a spell hits just right and sets off a chain reaction. All the necessary coincidences fall into place, and everything works out in such a spectacular way that witnesses are like, "How the heck did that happen?" This is my favorite thing in the whole world.

Other times, the spell lands, but the odds of success are too low for magic to make any difference. This does not mean that your Witchcraft is flawed, or that lust of result got the better of you. There were just too many variables in play for the spell to have any real influence.

Author and matchmaker Tracy McMillan once said, "Everything works out in the end; if it hasn't worked out yet, then it's not the end."[28] And this is applicable to magic along with relationships, especially when you're trying to find detours around variables to achieve the results you're working for.

Just remember that every spell makes a difference, and every possibility can be rerouted. And as a Chaos Witch, no magical operation is over until you say it is.

If it hasn't worked out yet, if the obstacles and variables have not been identified and circumvented, then you can rest assured that it's not the end.

---

28. McMillan, *I Love You and I'm Leaving You Anyway*, 7.

Discordian Dance Break
Seeing Is Believing

At some point in your Witchcraft career, you'll more than likely find yourself having to do some magic in which emotional investment is unavoidable: a spell to get your dream job; healing for your best friend; protection from bears; if bears are an issue in your area. In these moments, being really, really desperate for the magic to work will be a distraction and a detraction.

Luckily, I have a trick to overcome this. An excellent way to develop your potential for nonattachment is to cast spells for things in which you're *not* emotionally invested, so that you can get familiar with that mindset and recall it whenever necessary. Think of a simple desire (I say "desire" instead of "intent," because "desire" has a little more *oomph* to it), one that's specific but won't have any major impact on your life. For example: "Within three days, I will see a cherry-red convertible."

Write down your desire on a piece of paper and cross out all the repeating letters, which, in this case, leaves the following jumble:

WITHNRED
AYSLCOVB

Next, start moving the letters around in different sequences and arrangements, connecting them to each other, and letting your imagination take the wheel until you hit upon a design that seems right to you. Mine is a grumpy deep-sea creature refusing a generic sleep aid:

created it in the first place. But that's a good thing, because it means you're getting into a gnostic headspace.

Once your design is set, take a deep breath and blow vigorously onto it, fold it up, put it in your pocket, and move on with the rest of your day. Keep an eye out for red convertibles, and when you do see one, let that excitement bolster your own confidence in your magic. Trust that the spell will work, with your disengagement from the outcome playing a big part in that.

There's an unfounded but persistent concept out in Greater Pagandom that magic should only be used as a last resort, when all else fails. But magic is a craft, and just like any other extracurricular activity, time and effort are required to improve our skills—which we should be doing whenever we can, not just when we have to.

Having disciplined yourself, you'll be able to shift into nonattachment mode and practice quantitative Witchcraft to the best of your ability whenever you'd like. And when that happens, the results you need will be inevitable.

Principles of Chaos Witchcraft 73

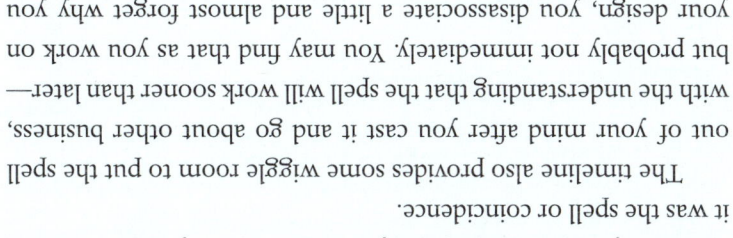

Convertible Sigil

Before we go any farther, let's take a step back and look at the desire itself. It is an improbable objective, but not an impossible one, and the specific color mentioned, along with the three-day timeline, magnifies the improbability. In other words, if the desire was just "I will see a red convertible," and you saw a brick-red convertible a year and a half later, you wouldn't really know whether it was the spell or coincidence.

The timeline also provides some wiggle room to put the spell out of your mind after you cast it and go about other business, with the understanding that the spell will work sooner than later—but probably not immediately. You may find that as you work on your design, you disassociate a little and almost forget why you

The Law of Fives

Guidelines and suggestions aside, there is one nonnegotiable law in Chaos Witchcraft. By this point, you may have noticed that the number five and multiples thereof have popped up a lot in this book: Eris was pregnant for fifty-five years and gave birth to five Elements; Order is represented by the five-sided pentagon; there are five seasons, each with seventy-three days (7+3=10); there are five Apostles, one of whom penned the Five Commandments; and if we count the introduction and conclusion, this book, published in 2025, has fifteen chapters.

This is all thanks to the Law of Fives, which is not really a principle per se. But it is a fundamental tenet of Discordianism, and as such, it deserves its own plug. According to the *Principia,* the Law of Fives states simply that "all things happen in fives, or are divisible by or are multiples of five, or are somehow directly or indirectly appropriate to five. The Law of Fives is never wrong."[29]

Astute readers will note that the word *five* appears five times in the passage, thus proving the Law of Fives.

On the surface, the Law of Fives appears to be a parody of scientific reliance on the number four—four Elements, four humors, four seasons, etc.—as well as a poke at the inherent obscenity of four-letter words. But the number five does historically, or at least mythologically, relate to Eris.

In his *Works and Days*, Hesiod wrote, "Beware of all the fifth days [of the month]; for they are harsh and angry; it was on the fifth, they say, that the Erinyes (Furies) assisted at the bearing of Horkos, whom Eris bore, to be a plague on those who take false oath."[30]

---

29. Hill and Thornley, *Principia Discordia*, 00016.
30. Atsma, "Horkos."

Whether or not the founders of Discordianism were aware of the connection between Eris and the fifth day of the month is anyone's guess, although it does bulk up the modern association with some nifty historical context. And even if the number was picked arbitrarily, the Law of Fives does provide us with an opportunity to control how we perceive the world around us—basically, you can make anything relate to the number five if you try hard enough.

For example, the number 23 is sacred within Discordianism, because 2+3=5. And the number 24 relates to the number 5, because 24–1=23, and 2+3=5. And the number 378 relates to 5, because 3+7+8=18, and 1+8=9, and 9 is only 1 number away from 10, which is a multiple of 5. And so on.

Making the conscious decision to see the number five everywhere we look is an example of controlling our beliefs, which is another step toward using those beliefs as tools. Although if you want to see Discordianism in real-world action, do some research on the 23 Enigma, which is a metaphysical theory that the number 23 is deeply but inexplicably significant. Digging into the 23 Enigma will yield stories that make the Law of Fives seem a lot more reasonable than anyone ever intended.

And here's the best part: From a practical Witchcraft standpoint, the Law of Fives is a Golden Ticket and Get Out of Jail Free Card rolled into one (or five).

How many herbs should you put in a charm bag? Five. How many nights should you light candles for your petitions? Five. How many times should you chant the words to a given spell? Five. How many days should you commit to a paradigm shift before deciding whether it's going to be valuable to your practice? Five. How many times should you text an unrequited crush before you accept that they're not going to text back? Five.

In 2024, I gave a presentation on Discordianism at an event called Austin Witchfest, and after I got through talking about the Law of Fives, an attendee raised his hand.

"We're in Room 5," he noted. "Did you pick this room on purpose?"

"I actually did not," I said, explaining that I was originally supposed to be in Room 1, but I'd received an email from the organizers on the Friday before the event, letting me know that the assignments had been rearranged, and I'd now be presenting in Room 5.

At which point another attendee spoke up: "So you found out you'd be in Room 5 … on the fifth day of the week."

"That is correct," I said.

And the whole room gasped like I'd just casually levitated.

They all may have shown up to my presentation as mild curiosity seekers, but they left as *believers*. As a Chaos Witch, this was really all I could have asked for.

Crafting with Chaos
Anointings Anonymous

Now that you're working on your nonattachment abilities, you can level up and start casting spells without knowing what spells you're casting.

Sounds fun, right? I think so too.

You will need

A plain carrier oil, such as almond or olive

Five identical tealights and/or papers

Aluminum foil and/or butcher paper

Directions

Think of a desire, and once it's fully formed in your mind, dab your finger in the oil and rub it in a circle around the top rim of one of the tealights—make a clockwise circle if the desire involves bringing something to you, and make a counterclockwise circle if the desire involves sending something away from you. Then wrap the tealight in aluminum foil or butcher paper (or anything nonabsorbent) and put it away. Do this with one of the tealights every night for five nights. Wait five more days, then select one of the candles and light it. Again, let your concentration settle on the work, not the outcome. Note any results.

Instead of candles, you can also write down a series of five simple desires and create a design for each one, like you did for the spell to see the red convertible. Once you've got a good selection of them, mix them up and set them aside for a week or so. After some time has passed, pull one at random, blow on it, and tear it up or burn it to release its potential. Repeat this every day with a different design, until you start getting comfortable with the work itself instead of the desire being the focus of your attention.

Chapter 6

The Chaos Star and Discordian Diamond

Picture an octopus. It can drastically change its appearance, and it can squeeze itself into almost anything. But regardless of what it happens to look like or where it happens to have hidden itself at any given moment, it is still, at its core, an octopus. That's because it has defining characteristics: Its adaptability and morphology, along with its ability to mimic whatever it wants, are the very things that fundamentally make it an octopus.

Just as you can look at an octopus in its original form and recognize it by its oval head and weird beak and eight tentacles, so too can we look at the overall shape and colors of Chaos Witchcraft to identify and understand how to apply it. To start, let's look at a star.

The Chaos Star

The design that came to be known as the Chaos Star was originally devised in the early 1960s by writer Michael Moorcock for his Elric of Melniboné stories. The symbol trickled from fiction to appear iconically in the *Warhammer* role-playing game, and it eventually wriggled its way into occultism, where it finally solidified as a symbol of Chaos Magic. It is also known as the Chaostar and the Sigil of Chaos, and if it's mapped out three-dimensionally, it's called a Chaosphere.

The Chaos Star

The Star does not really have a concrete meaning, although you can certainly extract a variety of interpretations out of it. The arrows can represent the eight points of the compass, or the symbol as a whole can represent the big bang, with matter and energy launching ballistically in all directions. Or you can look at it as a representation of Chaos itself, being the potential and momentum behind all action with no specific destination in mind, other than wherever you decide to take it.

The Colors

In *Liber Kaos*, Peter J. Carroll expands on the Star by adding color to the arrows to represent eight different forms of magic.[31] I've listed them with one notable change: Instead of associating green with love, I'm going to associate green with partnership (and I will talk about why a little later).

---

31. Carroll, *Liber Kaos*, 107–151.

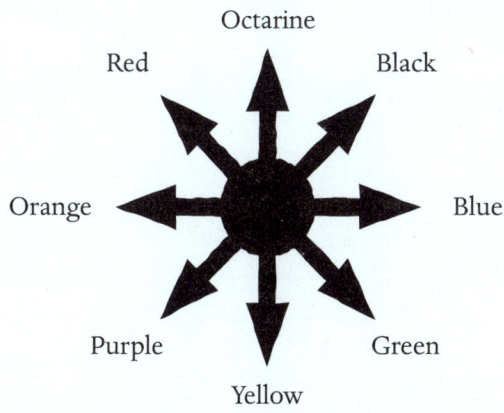

The Chaos Star with Colors Listed

Octarine—Pure Magic. The integration of the self and connection to the Divine, which Ceremonial Magicians call the Great Work. According to Sir Terry Pratchett in his Discworld series, octarine is a greenish yellow-purple that denotes the presence of magical energy. It is only visible to wizards and cats.[32]

Black—Death Magic. Necromancy, mediumship, and vampirism.

Blue—Wealth Magic. Money and prosperity.

Green—Partnership Magic. Developing and/or maintaining relationships, including those with plants and animals.

Yellow—Ego Magic. Knowledge, success, illumination, and illusions.

Purple—Sex Magic. Self-explanatory, but also Creation, creativity, and fertility.

---

32. Pratchett, *The Colour of Magic*, 32, 68.

Orange—Thinking Magic. Responsibility, strategy, travel, gambling, and risk-taking.

Red—War Magic. Conflict, defense, and protection.

If you're familiar with Hermetic Qabalah, you will notice that the colors of the arrows match those of the seven classical planets associated with the sepiroth, or spheres, of the Tree of Life. The difference, though, is that in a Qabalistic system, you'd be pathworking your way up the Tree, whereas in Chaos Magic, you can shoot off in whichever direction is most appropriate for the results you're trying to achieve.

How you use the colors of the Chaos Star is entirely up to you, and you can even choose to use them literally. For instance, if you were doing a ritual to protect investments, you might consider employing red and blue candles, cords, dyed oils, and so on in your work while invoking spirits of war and wealth. Or, since red + blue = purple, you could use Purple Magic to create opportunities for your investments to grow without interference.

The point here is that once you've got the structure of the colors down, you can do a lot of awesome stuff within it.

The Arrows

The arrows of the Star are not static, and in *Chaos Craft: The Wheel of the Year in Eight Colours*, authors Julian Vayne and Steve Dee rearrange the colors, while keeping the polarities intact, to align them with the contemporary Wiccan Sabbats, like so:

Octarine—Winter Solstice, sometimes called Yule (December 21)

Green—Imbolc (February 1)

Orange—Spring Equinox, sometimes called Ostara (March 21)

Purple—Beltane (May 1)

Yellow—Summer Solstice, sometimes called Litha (June 21)

Red—Lammas (August 1)

Blue—Autumnal Equinox, sometimes called Mabon (September 21)

Black—Samhain (November 1)

Within this paradigm, the magic being practiced corresponds to the cyclical celebrations. Since Lammas is a time of sacrifice, you could take the opportunity for a red ritual to venerate Mars (who is the plow as well as the sword); or, during Samhain, your magic would be black, in that it's the time to honor and commune with the dead. In these cases, the magic is bolstered by the season, making a Witch's work even more effective.

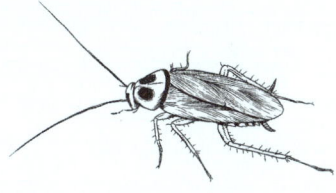

The Chaos Star and its eight magics is a perfectly actionable framework, and if you want to use it as the backbone of your own Chaos Witchcraft, you are more than welcome to do so. But nothing within Chaos Magic is set in stone, and there's no reason not to come up with your own way of categorizing magic that's unique to Chaos Witchcraft.

Discordian Dance Break

Barbarous Fnords

The word *fnord* first appeared on page 00010 of the *Principia* as a bit of amusing gibberish. However, Robert Anton Wilson and Robert Shea made use of the term in *The Illuminatus! Trilogy*, defining it as a written tool that creates a subconscious plant in a subject's mind. According to these novels, children are conditioned from an early age not to be able to see the word, so whenever it appears in print media, it causes discomfort and anxiety.[33] Therefore, shadowy organizations work to distribute the word throughout newspapers and magazine articles so that the unenlightened will be averse to reading about current events. But it is not used in any form of advertising, thus encouraging consumerism. Discordians use *fnord* as an all-purpose injection, exclamation, and expletive, again with no particular definition. But Wilson and Shea ascribed power to the word, which means that Chaos Witches can do the same.

Within the occult, a barbarous name is a nonsensical word that has no inherent meaning but becomes meaningful in a ritual context: The word transmits magic by how it is uttered and the force of will behind it.[34] Traditional Witches and Wiccans often end their spells with the phrase *so mote it be*, which translates to, "This spell will come to pass." Instead of ending your own spells with that phrase, try using *fnord* as a barbarous name and shouting it with all the intensity you can muster. Shift your beliefs so that the word means exactly what you want it to mean, and nothing less.

---

33. Wilson and Shea, *The Illuminatus! Trilogy*, 483–484.
34. Belanger, *The Dictionary of Demons*, 326.

Tidal Waves

In *Lid Off the Cauldron: A Handbook for Witches*, Patricia Crowther divides the Wheel of the Year into four seasonal tides: the Tide of Activation (from the Spring Equinox to the Summer Solstice), the Tide of Consolidation (from the Summer Solstice to the Autumn Equinox), the Tide of Recession (from the Autumn Equinox to the Winter Solstice), and the Tide of Lustration (from the Winter Solstice to the Spring Equinox). Crowther encourages Witches to keep the tides in mind—along with lunar phases and planetary positions—when planning the timing of magical workings, pointing out that the apex of each tide—and thus the most auspicious time for a corresponding magical operation—is one of the Greater Sabbats (Activation/Beltane, Consolidation/Lammas, Recession/Samhain, and Lustration/Imbolc).

If we want to bring some Traditional Witchcraft into our Chaos Witchcraft, we can capture the idea of seasonal tides, frappe it within a Chaos paradigm, and reinterpret it with the Discordian seasons. We can also look to the lesser-known *Honest Book of Truth* (the full text of which can be found in *Historia Discordia* by Adam Gorightly), in which Lord Omar described the Discordian seasons as Ages, to get an idea of how these tides might operate.

An Age of Chaos

"An Age of Chaos is one in which Things Seem Ready to Happen and, a midst much activity, no specific Direction seemeth yet to be emerging. These are Ages of Balance, wherein one action negates another in the Eye of the Observer, who does not yet exist."[35]

---

35. Gorightly, *Historia Discordia*, 181.

An Age of Discord

"An Age of Discord is one wherein Something Happens to Activate the Cycle of Events and the main theme of Whatever Is Coming begins to reveal Itself. These are also known as Primitive Ages, coming as they do after the Primal Ages of Chaos, and they are Ages of Unbalance as well."[36]

An Age of Confusion

"An Age of Confusion or an Ancient Age, is one in which History As We Know It begins to unfold, in which Whatever Is Coming emerges in Corporal Form, more or less, and such times are Ages of Balanced Unbalance, or Unbalanced Balance."[37]

An Age of Bureaucracy

"Age of Bureaucracy is an Imperial Age in which Things Mature, in which Confusion becomes entrenched, and during which Balanced Balance, or Stagnation, is attained."[38]

An Age of Aftermath

"An Age of Aftermath is an Apocalyptic Period of Transition back to Chaos through the Screen of Oblivion into which passeth, finally. These are the Ages of Unbalanced Balance."[39]

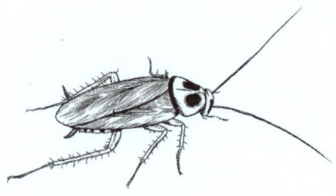

---

36. Gorightly, *Historia Discordia*, 181.
37. Gorightly, *Historia Discordia*, 181.
38. Gorightly, *Historia Discordia*, 181.
39. Gorightly, *Historia Discordia*, 181.

There are two ways to understand the tidal powers of the Discordian seasons. On one hand, you can time your magic to correspond with the Discordian calendar: For instance, a spell to get a promotion at work would represent maturation and could therefore be cast during the Season of Bureaucracy for maximum impact. On the other hand, you can think of the Discordian seasons not just *when* things can happen, but *how* those things can happen.

In other words, the Discordian seasons are distinct expressions of magic.

Diamonds Are a Discordian's Best Friend

How do the Discordian seasonal forms of magic relate to the eight forms of magic on the Chaos Star? Let's overlay them and find out.

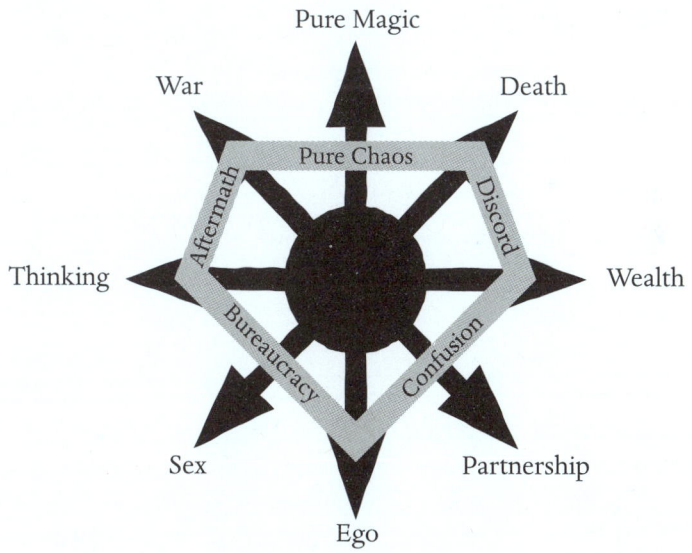

The Discordian Diamond

In this reimagining, the Discordian seasons are not set points, but spectrums around the Star. Discord, for example, connects death and wealth, whereas bureaucracy runs the gamut from ego to sex to thinking. And this means that we can use the seasons to complement—or even replace—the forms of magic symbolized by the Star. In fact, let's fall back on our Principle of Diverse Approaches, cull an idea from *Scottish Witchcraft: The History and Magick of the Picts* by Raymond Buckland, and apply it completely out of context to confirm our theory, "[W]e might say that there are five main headings for magick to be worked. These are: HEALTH, WEALTH, LOVE, PROTECTION, POWER."[40]

If we match those headings up with the Discordian seasons, update a couple of words, and take Lord Omar's Ages into account, we end up with the following:

Pure Chaos—Power

Discord—Fortune (we've already got wealth, plus fortune can be either good or bad)

Confusion—Love (this is why we changed green to partnership)

Bureaucracy—Health (a figurative or literal body's hierarchical systems of organization)

Aftermath—Protection

This leaves us with either five bonus forms of magic to add to the eight points of the Chaos Star, or five broad forms of magic that encompass the Chaos Star completely, both of which provide a robust configuration for Chaos Witchcraft. But because our emphasis is on experimenting with unfamiliar ideas, and because we've been rolling with Discordianism, I am going to focus on that second take.

---

40. Buckland, *Scottish Witchcraft*, 97.

Discordian Spells for All Occasions

Here are some examples of what Discordian Seasonal Magic can look like.

Pure Chaos Magic: Set Things in Motion

This is a spell of beginnings to be cast when you're preparing to start a new project or set off on an adventure. Perform this working so that things will fall into place for you.

You will need

    A white seven-day candle

    A black permanent marker

    Anointing oil

    A domino

Directions

On the side of the candle, use the marker to draw two arrows crashing into each other, shown here:

Dab your finger in the oil and touch the top of the candle five times, like pips on a die: twice above the wick, once at the base of the wick, and twice below it. On a table, or on your altar if you have one, set the domino on end. Imagine a series of events, like a movie montage, leading up to the result you're trying to accomplish. Once those events are clear in your mind, light the candle, then pick it up with both hands. Use the base of the candle to knock over the domino. Let the candle burn down. See what happens.

Discord Magic: The Stench of Success

This is a spell to tip fortune in your favor, to bring in some extra money or resources when needed, and to help that income grow.

You will need

    A strong-smelling incense, such as nag champa

    A bay leaf

    A blue or green scented marker

    Your favorite cologne

Directions

Light the incense. Take a moment to savor the fragrance. Pick up the bay leaf, hold it close to your face, and inhale deeply. Using the marker, draw a symbol of wealth on the bay leaf—this could be a dollar sign, the astrological symbol of Jupiter, a sigil of your own creation, or a combination of all.

Hold the bay leaf over the incense, letting the smoke curl over both sides. Spritz the bay leaf with cologne, then take another whiff of the leaf, inhaling deeply through your nose. Exhale through your mouth, blowing your desire onto the leaf.

Bury the leaf by your front door. Wear the cologne for the next five days.

Confusion Magic: Sticky-Sweet Glamour

A glamour is a spell that changes how the Witch who casts it appears to the people around them. This glamour is intended to increase your confidence and draw favorable attention.

You will need

A bathtub

A can of Dr Pepper

A small paper heart

Directions

Remove your clothes and get comfortable in the tub. Hold the can of Dr Pepper to your forehead and concentrate on how you want to be perceived, and what kind of attention you want to attract. Once you feel ready, crack open the Dr Pepper, take a sip, and slowly pour it over yourself, feeling the twenty-three flavors bubbling and sticking to you, like an additional layer of skin that you can reshape however you'd like. Finish up by bathing as you normally would. Recycle the can with the paper heart inside.

Bureaucracy Magic: Bound and Gagged

Outside of the occult, the word *bureaucracy* is synonymous with red tape, which is the inspiration behind this binding spell. Cast it to bog down or otherwise prevent a given something or someone from reaching you.

You will need

A poseable doll or action figure representative of your target[41]

Water

Masking tape

---

[41]. If you can't find a toy that strikes you as appropriate for the working, go with a general classic cartoon foil, like Elmer Fudd or Yosemite Sam.

Directions
Name the toy after your target. If you *really* want to go big, you can perform an entire baptismal rite out of *The Book of Common Prayer* like they did in the novel *The Witches of Eastwick* by John Updike. But if you're cramped for time, just dab a little water on the doll's forehead and say, "By Bureaucracy made, by Bureaucracy changed. You are not [whatever the toy is made from], but flesh and blood. I name you [name of target]. You are they."

Take your masking tape and wrap it haphazardly around the toy five times, with the majority of the tape going around the arms and legs. Once the poppet is trussed up to your liking, place it in the very back of your freezer, using whatever else you happen to have in there to create a blockade around it.

Aftermath Magic: Defensive Optic Blast

This is a pop culture twist on a talisman meant to ward off the Evil Eye. Keep it near the front of your home to boost protection.

You will need

- An iron nail
- A small orange bag
- A picture of your favorite superhero with vision- or light-based powers (Superman, Cyclops, Dazzler, etc.)
- Red thread
- Hot sauce

Directions
Place the iron nail at the bottom of the bag. Gaze at the picture of the superhero, making eye contact with the image, then fold it five times and slide it into the bag as well. Use the thread to tie off the

bag with five knots. Anoint both sides of the bag with a drop of hot sauce, then hang it in a visible location. Warning: Wash your hands before touching your eyes.

Crafting with Chaos
Customizing Your Colors

There's absolutely nothing wrong with using prefab color correspondences, but since Chaos Witchcraft is experimental by nature, you are free to come up with your own to see how they work for you. Here's a way to give that a whirl.

On a sheet of paper, write down the following:

Your least favorite color.

A color you associate with opulence.

The color that looks best on you.

A color you wear when you want to be taken seriously (your power color).

A sensual color—or, alternatively, a color you associate with creativity.

A color that makes you think of a finish line.

A color that makes you angry.

Your favorite color.

What you have created, then, is a set of colors that keys into each form of magic on the Chaos Star in your own terms. As an example, here are my colors: salmon, crimson, navy blue, charcoal, fuchsia, white, burnt orange, aqua. For me, these resonate as death (salmon), wealth (crimson), partnership (navy blue), ego (charcoal), sex (fuchsia), thinking (white), war (burnt orange), and Pure Magic (aqua).

Now, try this exercise again, but this time with a shorter list of criteria:

A garish color.

A color that clashes with the garish color.

The color of your favorite dessert.

A healthy color.

A color that makes you feel safe.

What you are left with is a set of colors specifically relating to the Discordian forms of magic. Mine are neon yellow, grey, pumpkin, forest green, chartreuse. For me, this means Pure Chaos (neon yellow), discord (grey), confusion (pumpkin), bureaucracy (forest green), and aftermath (chartreuse).

These color stories can be used when picking out candles for spellwork, or when choosing particular inks with which to draw sigils. You may find that one color fills multiple slots—maybe your favorite color also happens to be the color that looks best on you. And that's okay! There's absolutely nothing saying that we can't utilize a single color for more than one magical purpose. This is all about what works for you in your practice, not what works for anyone else in theirs.

And if you can't come up with a color for every association, or you don't want to rely on correspondences at all, I promise that's okay too. In this case, we can fall back on one of the fundamental maxims of fashion:

Beige goes with everything.

Chapter 7
Sigils, Servitors, and Symbols

The Chaos approach can really be applied to any magical practice, although there are some techniques developed by early Chaos Magicians—specifically those involving the creation of sigils and servitors—that eventually found their way into the occult mainstream. And that has resulted in a bit of stagnation, especially when Witches started to believe that these techniques could not be altered or amended in any way.

Let me be clear: When it comes to the Creative processes of Chaos Witchcraft, there are no correct ways to do anything. There are ways of doing things that may prove more effective than others, but ultimately, whatever you're doing only has to work for *you*. If you are getting the results you want, no one can tell you that your methods are wrong.

There are also a metric frackton of resources out there regarding sigils and servitors, so with some digging, you are all but guaranteed to find systems that work perfectly for you. And hey, if you don't, you can always do what the original Chaotes did and invent your own. In fifty years, maybe some hardcore Chaos dude will be swearing to his friends that the method you devised is the *only* way to make sigils.

Sigils

Within Chaos Magic and Chaos Witchcraft, a sigil is a visual representation of a desire, created to bring that desire into reality. The most recognizable method of sigilization was originally devised by Austin Osman Spare and refined by Ray Sherwin, and I touched on it in the Discordian Dance Break in chapter 5 (page 71). Using this method, you will write down your desire, cross out repeating letters, then play around with the arrangement of the letters until you come up with an integrated design that incorporates all of them.

Pictorial Sigils

At its core, a sigil is a symbol of a desired outcome, but we don't necessarily have to write out that desire to get results. We can 100 percent draw it instead.

Pictorial sigils are sympathetic in nature. The Witch sketches out a depiction of what they want to see happen, and then that image is broken down and consolidated into a simple, abstract motif—one that represents their goal just as emphatically as a sigil created with letters would. It's a very "as above, so below" kind of working, and it lends itself to a lot of expressiveness and originality.

And please note that you don't have to be a talented artist to pull this off: A stick figure drawing would honestly make a more practical template for a pictorial sigil than a fine art portrait, because the overall design would be a lot more straightforward and pliable.

I generally have not had a lot of success with pictorial sigils, but I've also found a method that does work for me. If other systems of sigil creation haven't done much for you in the past, give pictorial sigils a try and see what results you can generate.

Scrigils

This is my all-time favorite method of sigil generation, and I have never gotten anything but spectacular results from it. Plus, it's incredibly simple: Grab a pen and a piece of paper, clear your mind, close your eyes, think about your desire, then pick up the pen and let your hand gently start moving it around the paper, in whatever direction it wants to go.

Let your desire play out like a movie, audiobook, or tasting menu while your hand meanders, until the story organically comes to its conclusion. Stop drawing. Open your eyes and admire your new scrigil.

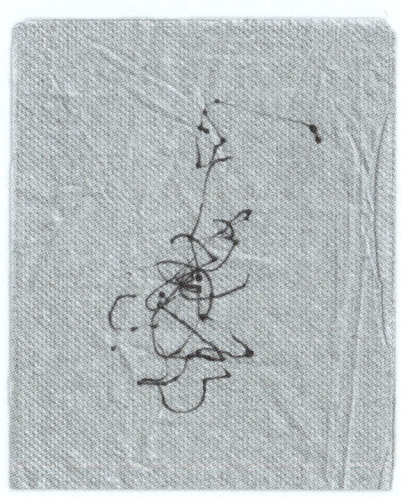

A Scribbled Sigil on a Jack in the Box Napkin.
Photo provided by author

I honestly couldn't tell you why this method works so well for me, but the spells I've cast using scrigils have always hit their marks. If this ends up not being your thing, no worries—you've got plenty of other options from which to choose.

Charging and Firing

So, you've got your sigil (or scrigil) ready, and it's time to move forward. Here's what to do to fully cast your spell.

Sit comfortably, with your back straight and your feet touching the floor. Hold your sigil in front of you, keeping your eyes focused on it. Take a deep breath, and, starting with your feet, tighten your muscles as hard as you can, feeling that tightness move up your body, until every muscle is clenched. Hold this for as long as possible. Once you can't keep clenched any longer, relax and exhale sharply, blowing all the air in your lungs onto the sigil.

Repeat this procedure two more times. I would normally say four more times to keep things in line with the Law of Fives, but I also don't want you to hyperventilate. After the third expulsion of air onto your sigil, it will be charged.

The next step is to fire it—the method of which will depend on the form of magic aligned with the goal of your spellwork: If the spell is Pure Chaos or Aftermath Magic, the sigil should be burned. If the spell is Confusion or Bureaucracy Magic, the sigil should be buried. If the spell is Discord Magic, the sigil can either be burned or buried, on a case-by-case basis.

Discordian Dance Break

A Better Word

Okay, let's take our foot off the gas for a second. Within the realm of occult how-to books, you will often come across the word *visualize*, which means "to see something in your mind's eye": Visualize the results of your spell, or visualize the person you want to be. Basically, picture it.

Thing is, not everyone *can* picture it. People with aphantasia—the inability to visualize—don't see mental pictures at all. But this does not mean that they can't practice Witchcraft, nor should any of us be solely dependent on mental images for our spells to work.

Eris gave us five senses, and since input to any of them can trigger memories, all of them can be used to create imaginary depictions of the events we want to make happen. You have just as much potential to hear or feel or taste or smell your desire as you do to see it, so instead of lumping all those skills under the misnomer of *visualization*, let's group them under a more accurate and inclusive word: *foretelling*. When you're casting a spell, foretell the results you want to achieve, using whichever senses make the most sense to you.

Verbal Sigils

One of the first occult books I ever bought was *The Magick of Chant-O-Matics* by Raymond Buckland. It's as campy as the title suggests, and very much a product of its time, but it did get me in the habit of actively stating my desires out loud when doing spellwork. Verbal sigils are not a far leap from this concept.

To create verbal sigils, you can start with the standard sigil creation method, but instead of combining letters into a singular glyph, rearrange them to create a short chant or mantra. For instance, if you take the letters from a phrase like *I have all the money I need to afford a vacation*, you can produce any number of verbal sigils:

> CORF LATH MINDEV
>
> FEVCIN HARF MOLT
>
> LECT FINDAH VROM
>
> HI, VORM? CAD LEFT!

Verbal sigils may be worked into rituals or spells however you see fit. But in keeping with the innovations of Chaos Witchcraft, you might want to try something completely unorthodox with them, like standing on a median and shouting them five times into oncoming traffic.

Hypersigils

Comic book legend Grant Morrison originally coined the term *hypersigil* in reference to their series *The Invisibles*, the plotline of which was charged to bring about changes in Morrison's reality: As the story evolved and developed, so did Morrison. A hypersigil works on the same principles as a regular sigil, in that it's a symbolic representation of a desire. However, the difference between the two is that a hypersigil is fourth-dimensional; instead of being a static image, it has a narrative quality that propels it through time. It's kind of like writing fanfic about yourself. Morrison explains it a lot better than I can.

"The hypersigil can take the form of a poem, a story, a song, a dance, or any other extended artistic activity you wish to try. This is a newly developed technology so the parameters remain to be explored… The hypersigil is a dynamic miniature model of the Magician's universe, a hologram, microcosm or 'voodoo doll' which can be manipulated in real time to produce changes in the macrocosmic environment of 'real' life."[42]

The comic series *Promethea* presents a good example of hypersigils at work. In those books, whenever someone writes a poem or a story about Promethea, she appears in the real world to fight evil. There's a lot more to the story than just that, of course, but the gist is that Promethea is summoned by creative endeavors, which can serve as a bit of inspiration as you explore the concept of hypersigils yourself.

And as you are poking around, keep in mind that social media provides a wealth of hypersigil potential. Consider a blog in which the author writes from the perspective of who they want to be, versus who they currently are. An entire backstory could be crafted, with posts detailing, say, everything they did that day at their dream job, or where they're going for a romantic dinner with their idealized, yet-to-have-been-introduced partner.

Consider the filters that alter photos however the user wishes, or the apps that allow you to film and edit videos. In fact, try this:

---

42. Morrison, "Pop Magic!"

1. Sigilize a desire using the verbal sigil technique described earlier in this chapter.
2. Put together a video using your preferred app. The topic of the video can be whatever you'd like.
3. Add a text box, then type in the words from your verbal sigil.
4. Slide the text box offscreen. It will not be visible to your audience, but it will remain part of the post.
5. Add any captions or hashtags relevant to the subject of the video, then post it.

And with that, you will have set a hypersigil loose on the internet, and every like, favorite, and share it receives will increase its power. The video can be deleted once your results have been achieved.

Cut-Ups

If you're old enough to remember when *The Secret* was all the rage, then you probably also remember when vision boards were trending: big pieces of poster board that people would decorate with words and phrases clipped from magazines, along with stock photos that corresponded to whatever desires they were trying to passively manifest.

In theory, cut-ups are similar to vision boards, although in practice, they're a lot more like ransom notes. In either case, a cut-up is basically a collage, assembled with a specific magical goal in mind.

**Devotional Cut-Up to Anteros,
Personification of Requited Love, by Scott Woodward**

A cut-up can be simple or intricate, incorporating as many different words, symbols, and images as you see fit. And a cut-up does not have to be limited to the visual: William Burroughs was known to create audio cut-ups by splicing different sound recordings together—essentially creating an esoteric mix tape—then playing them out loud at the location where he wanted to see the effects of his magic. Burroughs also employed cut-ups as a literary technique, slicing up a written work into individual words, mixing them, and rearranging them at random to create new poems. You can use this method as well, cutting sentences out of magazines or print newspapers, breaking them down to individual words or letters, then placing them into a greater collage in whatever sequence makes sense to your deep mind.

My only firm suggestion is that the size of the cut-up should be appropriate to the work you're doing with it. If you're making a cut-up for a single spell, it really shouldn't be any bigger than a standard index card. If the cut-up is devotional in nature—assembled as an effigy of a particular deity, or to be used as an altar backdrop—then the cut-up can be made with a base of poster board, or even decoupaged on a wall. This example is a devotional cut-up to Anteros—the personification of requited love, by Scott Woodward.

Regardless of what its purpose will be, the cut-up should always appeal to your personal aesthetic sensibilities: You should like how it looks, and you should like looking at it. And this is important, because if you created it for a one-shot spell, you're going to charge and fire the cut-up like you would a sigil—which means destroying it. And that can be a hard thing to do, which makes it a sacrifice. And that Destructive sacrifice will add Creative power to your magic.

Servitors

In the short horror stories he penned for the magazine *Weird Tales* in the 1930s, author Clark Ashton Smith referred to the undead minions of Sorcerers as *servitors*.[43] And at some indeterminable

---

43. Smith, "The Empire of the Necromancer," 338–344.

point, the word floated into Chaos Magic, where it was used to describe a semi-independent thoughtform constructed to perform a specific task.

Think of a servitor as a noncorporeal extension of yourself, with just enough agency to do its job without supervision while remaining under your full control. A servitor can be created for any reason, although there are some things to consider before you set about forging one of your own. These factors are foundation, purpose, programming, appearance, identity, lifespan, and activation. Let's look at them individually.

Foundation

If we're going to build anything, we need something on which to construct it. Think about the Discordian Elements as described in chapter 2: Which of the five relates to your servitor? If its primary goal is going to be, say, increasing wealth, which corresponds with Discord Magic, you'll want to focus on Pungent; if it will act as a guardian, you'll be drawing on Aftermath Magic, so the servitor will be built on Orange.

Purpose

The purpose of your servitor is basically the same as the desire or intent behind a spell. On a clean sheet of paper, write out that desire as a directive. For example, "Help me bring in more money." Or, "Keep solicitors and door-to-door salespeople away from my home."

Programming

So now that you have a solid idea of your servitor's magical foundation and specific purpose, you can start collecting symbols that resonate with the job you want the servitor to do, which will be used in the activation process.

You can create a sigil, or a scrigil, or bring in numerology or planetary glyphs, or anything else that would reinforce the purpose of the servitor. Combine those images however you'd like into one comprehensive metasigil that feels right to you, and add that final design to the paper under the purpose.

Appearance

Your servitor can take on any form you'd like, but for the sake of Chaos Witchcraft, you can draw inspiration from the Element providing its foundation: an animated cloud of smoke for Pungent, a glowing orb for Orange, and so on. Or, if you're up for it, you can also go crazy with details.

I once made a servitor that looked like a softball-sized blue bumblebee, but I've made others that are just swirling balls of light. It's likely no one other than you will ever see the servitor, so however you want it to appear is completely valid.

Identity

What (or if) you decide to name your servitor is also completely up to you, although a memorable name will help reinforce its mission. One way to come up with a name is to create a verbal sigil based on the servitor's purpose. "Help me bring in more money" could give us the following options:

Brimple Yongh

Gin Hopelbrym

Limb Boy Phren (Which would also be a good name for a pop-punk garage band.)

Lifespan

Length of existence is definitely something to consider when mapping out a servitor. If it's only going to have a single one-shot responsibility, and you won't need it after that task is complete, then it really doesn't need to exist much longer than that. However, if you need it to consistently or repeatedly do a job, you'll want to make sure it lasts indefinitely. In which case, take some time to think about what will fuel it and keep it going.

You may also want to introduce a killswitch—that is, a particular action that will immediately end the servitor's existence, like saying its name backward. This really isn't a safety precaution so much as it is (for lack of a better way of saying it) euthanasia. Once all its jobs are complete, you don't want it just floating sadly around without a purpose. Have some mercy and put the little guy down.

Something else to think about is *where* your servitor will live. If there will be periods of inactivity between the times you call on it, a home base is not a bad idea: a statue, or a piece of jewelry, or even a part of your body.

Activation

Once you've got every aspect of your servitor in mind, write it all down, then read this list of attributes out loud. You can use the following as a template:

> *Your name is [name of servitor], and you exist to [state purpose here].*
> *You are charged with the following abilities.*
> *[List off everything you want your servitor to be able to do, including how it will move around (levitation, flight, teleportation, etc.), whether it can learn by doing, and whether it can change its own shape, size, appearance, and visibility as needed to accomplish its goals.]*

> *You gain strength from my awareness of you,*
> *and from my appreciation of your efforts.*
>
> *You will always come to me when I call your name,*
> *or whenever I need you.*
>
> *Your abilities will increase every time you*
> *successfully complete a task for me.*
>
> *You will live [indefinitely, or until a particular date].*
>
> *If I, and only I, [insert your killswitch here],*
> *you will immediately dissipate, and your energy will return to me.*
>
> *You are born on [date and time of the working],*
> *when your sigil is charged and fired.*

Charge and fire the sigil, and that's it! You've officially birthed a servitor. Congratulations on the latest addition to your family.

The Five-Fingered Hand of Eris

I have one final symbol that I want to discuss: the Five-Fingered Hand of Eris. Mentioned in the Pure Chaos spell in chapter 6, the Five-Fingered Hand of Eris, from an aesthetic standpoint, has always been one of my favorite occult symbols.

The Hand first appeared on page 00021 of the *Principia*, accompanied by the following text:

> The official symbol of POEE [Paratheo-Anametamystik-hood Of Eris Esoteric] is here illustrated. It may be this, or any similar device to represent TWO OPPOSING ARROWS CONVERGING INTO A COMMON POINT. It may be vertical, horizontal, or else such, and it may be elaborated or simplified as desired.
>
> NOTE: In the lore of western magic, the [crescent moon] is taken to symbolize horns, especially the horns of

Satan or of diabolical beasties. The Five Fingered Hand of Eris, however, is not intended to be taken as satanic, for the "horns" are supported by another set of inverted "horns". Or maybe it is walrus tusks. I don't know what it is, to tell the truth.[44]

The Five-Fingered Hand of Eris

The *Principia* doesn't ascribe any further meaning to the Hand, although for some Discordians, it's come to represent the forces of Creation and Destruction crashing into each other. There was a (surprisingly successful) push to get it recognized as the official astronomical symbol of the dwarf planet Eris, but other than that, it just kind of means "Discordian." As a sigil, though, I feel like it also has some magical uses.

Astronomical Symbol for the Dwarf Planet Eris

Are you familiar with the Hand of Glory? Back in the olden days, it was a candle made out of the severed left hand and the rendered fat of a hanged convict. When lit, the Hand of Glory was

---

44. Hill and Thornley, *Principia Discordia*, 00021.

believed to paralyze anyone in its vicinity, and it could also open any locked door.[45] You can see a Hand of Glory in action in the original *Wicker Man* (1973).

My theory is that if a Hand of Glory caused bodies at rest to remain motionless, the Five-Fingered Hand of Eris could be used to set things in motion.

If I wanted to engineer a series of events that would culminate in a specific goal, I would cast the Pure Chaos spell on page 89, grabbing a seven-day candle, drawing a Hand of Eris down the front of it, anointing it with oil, and, if I was feeling saucy, dressing it with the herb five-finger grass (to activate the handiness, and also because the name is on the nose), along with any other herbs and oils relevant to the work. And then I could go ahead with the spell as described.

Crafting with Chaos
Moon Water

As popular as it is to make moon water by leaving a jar of water on a windowsill during the full moon, I have to admit that I'm not a fan. Technically, all water is *already* moon water: The gravitational pull of the moon controls the tides, and since our bodies are around 60 percent water, the moon can have a profound effect on our mood, mental health, and temperament. We don't have to make the water more moonish to use it in magic.

The keyword here, of course, is *use*. If we're going to take the time to make something, we should do stuff with it. And there's another form of lunar water that has several practical uses, both magical and mundane.

---

45. "Hand of Glory."

The willow tree has long been associated with water and the moon. It's a quick-rooting plant that thrives along the banks of bodies of water. Additionally, willow is rich in a chemical called salicin, a natural anti-inflammatory and fever reducer that has been used in medicine for thousands of years. If you want to make a moon-oriented libation, willow water is an excellent way to go.

Willow water can be sipped as a headache remedy (although it's got a bitter taste, so best not to chug—at least maybe add some honey), or it can be used in a relaxing and/or ritual bath. Or, it can be poured as an offering to the moon—a lot of gardeners swear that soaking a new plant's roots in willow water before potting will help it flourish, so we can symbolically capitalize on this by pouring our willow water at the base of a tree (oaks are sacred to Diana, so that would be a good choice), or using it to nourish anything we plant on the full moon, either physically or metaphysically.

Making willow water from scratch is not too much of an onus, provided you've got willow trees nearby, or you have access to willow twigs. However, in a pinch, you can make bootleg willow water with a humble Bayer aspirin, which is honestly the more Chaos Witchcraft approach.

The active ingredient in aspirin is salicylic acid, which is a synthetic derivative of the salicin found in willow. Dissolve an aspirin in a cup of water, and you have kitbashed willow water. The salicylic acid is just as beneficial to root systems as willow water is, so you can still pour it as an offering. Plus, from a symbolic perspective, what is a round, white, willowy pill if not a tiny moon?

You will need

The full moon

A needle or toothpick

An aspirin

A bottle of water

Directions

On the night of the full moon, create a sigil for the desire of your choice. Astrologically, the moon stays full for three days—that is, if the full moon falls on a Saturday, you can still do full moon work on Friday or Sunday—so that gives you some extra breathing room to pull this off.

Once your sigil is ready, use your needle or toothpick to carve your sigil onto the aspirin. It doesn't need to be perfect or cut deeply into the pill—just an impression of it will do. Use the method described on page 98 to charge the sigil. After that, drop the inscribed aspirin into the bottle of water, cap it, and give it a good shake, thus firing the sigil. Set the bottle aside but check on it every thirty-five minutes or so, shaking it each time until the pill is fully dissolved.

How you employ your sigilized willow water depends on the spell you're casting. If the sigil you created is for protective Aftermath Magic, for instance, pour the water along the boundary of your home; if the sigil is to improve your dating options, add the water to a tea brewed with love-oriented herbs like lavender and vanilla and sip it while watching your favorite romantic comedy.

It may take some patience and a little exertion, but the satisfaction that comes from being able to say "I legitimately made this" is worth it. And really, as a Chaos Witch, you can't be afraid of putting that extra effort into your craft. Don't be afraid of getting your hands wet.

Chapter 8
Daemons, Demons, and Pop Culture Chaos

Despite being crafted as a parody religion, many Discordians—including its founders—came to accept the bona fide existence of Eris. As Mal-2 stated when Margot Adler interviewed him for *Drawing Down the Moon*, "If you do this type of thing well enough, it starts to work." He also added that Lord Omar once confided, "If I had realized that all of this was going to come *true*, I would have chosen Venus."[46]

Mal-2 himself did not originally believe in Eris—he just found it hysterical that the Greeks had a goddess of discord and thought it would be funny if there was a religion devoted to her. But over time, his perception of the deity changed. "Eris is an authentic goddess," he told Adler. "Furthermore, she is an old one."[47] While Mal-2 never identified as a Chaos Magician, his experience with Eris is a prime example of how Chaos Magic tends to operate: His practice developed first, and his beliefs evolved to accommodate them.

As a Chaos Witch, you are free to believe in whatever—or whomever—you'd like. But aside from the

---

46. *Drawing Down the Moon*, 336.

47. *Drawing Down the Moon*, 336.

standard gods and goddesses who appear in world mythologies, there are a myriad of other entities floating around out there who are worthy of veneration. Some may have more fictional origins than others, but all of them are as real as you allow them to be.

Principles Personified

Although generally referred to as a goddess, Eris was perceived as a daemon in ancient Greek religion and philosophy: That is, she was understood to be a personification of an abstract concept. Roughly one hundred fifty different personifications appear in Greek mythology and literature, representing a variety of notions, such as Love, Grief, Age, Hunger, Modesty, Persuasion, Fame, Rivalry, Peace, and Injustice.

For the most part, personifications were not worshiped or venerated in the same way the Olympians and related gods were. But there is nothing saying that you can't invoke one or more of them to bolster the magical work you're doing.

In addition to Eris, here are some other personifications you might consider calling upon as a Chaos Witch, each of which can be tied to a particular Chaos principle, form of magic, or Discordian Element. If you ever hit a mental block with one of these concepts, reach out to the corresponding personification and see if they can shed some light for you.

- **Akratos**—Personification of Unmixed Wine. He is associated with Sweet.
- **Dolos**—Personification of Guile and Craftiness. He is associated with Diverse Approaches.
- **Dysnomia**—Personification of Lawlessness. She is associated with Avoidance of Dogma.

Epidotes—Personification of Ritual Purification. She is associated with Deconditioning.

Eutychia—Personification of Good Luck. She is associated with Orange.

Homonoia (not to be confused with Harmonia/Aneris)—Personification of Unanimity and Oneness of Mind. She is associated with Partnership.

Hygeia—Personification of Good Health. She is associated with Prickle.

Hypnos—Personification of Sleep and the Father of Dreams. He is associated with Gnosis.

Iakkhos—Personification of the Ritual Shout. He is associated with Boom.

Kairos—Personification of Opportunity. He is associated with Thinking.

Lethe—Personification of Forgetfulness; also the name of the underworld river from which spirits of the recently deceased drink to forget their previous incarnations. She is associated with Immersion.

Nike—Personification of Victory. She is associated with Ego.

Pheme (sometimes called **Ossa**)—Personification of Rumor, Reputation, and Scandal. She is associated with Pungent.

Ploutos—Personification of Agricultural Bounty. He is associated with Wealth.

Polemos—Personification of Battle. He is associated with War.

Pothos—Personification of Sexual Desire. He is associated with Sex.

Sophia—Personification of Wisdom. She is associated with Personal Experience.

> **Sophrosyne**—Personification of Self-Control. She is associated with Discipline.
>
> **Tekhne**—Personification of Technical Skill. She is associated with Technical Excellence.
>
> **Thanatos**—Personification of Nonviolent Death. He is associated with Death.

And of course, if there's not already a cohesive personification of the condition, emotion, or quality you want to evoke, you can do what Hesiod (allegedly) did and simply make one up. Or else you can revamp your beliefs and start worshiping fictional characters.

Discordian Demonolatry

There's a line in the Old Testament that reads, "For all the gods of the Gentiles are demons," from which stems the idea that the gods of one religion are the demons of the next.[48] That is certainly one way to approach the concept of demons, although contemporary demonolater Ramsey Dukes offers an alternative view: As he sees it, demons are the personifications of the trials, frustrations, and microaggressions of daily life.[49]

Both perceptions are valid, and my own thoughts on demons ping-pong between the two. But for the purposes of Chaos Witchcraft, I want you to consider Dukes's take—if the Greek personifications offer illumination, demons can offer pathways around the obstacles they represent.

At some point in the 1980s, Lord Omar reached out to Discordian artist and musician Roldo Odlor and presented the rough outline of a book containing information on the demonic inhabitants of Thud. (*Thud* being Lord Omar's name for the real world, which

---

48. Psalm 95:5 (Catholic Public Domain Version).
49. Dukes, *Uncle Ramsey's Little Book of Demons*, 3.

is intriguing, considering that Zarathud is the Apostle of Bureaucracy, the season most related to earthly matters.) Roldo sketched some designs for the demons and sent them back to Lord Omar, and although the two lost touch, Roldo hung on to the originals, which were, almost two decades later, published alongside Lord Omar's descriptions as the *Goetia Discordia*.

The *Goetia* does not offer much in the way of ritual instruction, but based on their portrayals, the demons themselves are very much personifications in their own right. Relations with them would come in handy whenever you find yourself having to navigate the more Aneristic aspects of our society.

There are nine demons described in the *Goetia*. Here are eight of them:

> **Babbity**—Demon of Unoriginality.
>
> **Evangelicus**—Demon of Dogma.
>
> **Filibuster**—Demon of Gossip.
>
> **Flagstone**—Demon of Mindlessness and Obedience.
>
> **Grimpil**—Demon of Diversity Prevention.
>
> **Starbuck**—Demon of Superstitions.
>
> **Technocrust**—Demon of Redundancy.
>
> **Uncle Albert**—Demon of Dress Codes and Consumerism.[50]

The ninth demon of the *Goetia* is Azazel. He stands out a bit since he's the only one to make significant appearances in religions outside of Discordianism. As such, he deserves some special attention.

Azazel

In Judaism, Azazel is the goat who carries collective sins out of the community; in apocryphal Christianity and ceremonial magic, he's

---
50. Thornley and Odlor, *Goetia Discordia*.

a fallen angel who taught humankind the arts of cosmetics, metalworking, and Witchcraft; and in Islam, he's one of three angels who were picked to go to Earth and live among mortals, although he changed his mind at the last minute and went back to heaven.[51] But in Discordianism, Azazel guards the exit out of Thud.

The *Goetia* describes Azazel as having a masculine human body and the face of a prophet, with a serpent in place of his left arm.[52] It also states that he cannot be summoned, only encountered unexpectedly, and that he holds the Apple of Discord in his right hand. To get past him, the apple must be filled out in triplicate.

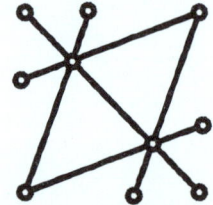

Heinrich Cornelius Agrippa's Seal of Saturn,
Which, Over Time, Has Become Known as the Sigil of Azazel

Lord Omar did not explain why he chose this particular imagery, but it's not too hard to unlock a deeper meaning. When you are presented with an opportunity to engage in Creative Disorder, you are interacting with Azazel. And the more Creative Disorder you incite or inspire, the more filled out his apple becomes. Eventually, he will step aside and allow you to pass, at which time you'll see beyond the grids of Order and Disorder, getting a glimpse of reality itself.

Which is a lot to process, but definitely worth imagining.

---

51. Belanger, *The Dictionary of Demons*, 80–81.

52. Goetia Discordia, 21–22.

Discordian Dance Break

A Superstitious Lot

My mother was as pragmatic as they come, and she did not indulge in irrationality of any kind … except when it came to pennies. "Find a penny, pick it up," she'd exclaim whenever she happened to spot a random copper coin on the ground. "And all the day, you'll have good luck!" And this is where her repressed superstitious upbringing kicked into high gear, because the maxim only applied to pennies that were faceup. Tails-up pennies were bad luck and had to stay where they were, *or else*. They could, however, be turned over, so that whoever came across them next could benefit from auspiciousness.

From this, I learned that every superstition has a remedy, and every one of those remedies is a potential apotropaic aftermath spell.

If you accidentally walk under a ladder, all you have to do is walk under it again, but backward this time; if you break a mirror, just wait seven hours to collect the pieces, and you won't have to deal with those pesky seven years of bad luck; spilling salt is ominous, but throwing a pinch of it over your shoulder averts any sodium-related disasters.

Upon learning that a given practice is closed and/or initiatory, a common complaint from younger Witches of European descent is, "Well, then what am I supposed to do? My culture doesn't have any magic." But it does! There is cultural magic all around us in local superstitions and folk beliefs. The more of them you collect in your area, the more unique regional magic will be accessible to you. Ask Starbuck, the demon of superstition, to guide you on your quest.

Granted, I live in Texas, so the majority of our superstitions revolve around our sports franchises. Plus our minor league hockey team—the only team I really cared about—relocated to Des Moines in 2013. But I flip at least five pennies a week, so I've still got a rich well of cultural magic from which to draw.

The Original Snake Oil Salesman

Be they daemonic or demonic, personifications are fairly easy to get one's brain around, but you may find yourself pushing back when confronted with a more nebulous concept—something like pop culture deities. And this is completely understandable. Rest assured, though, that pop culture deities have historical precedence with modern-day application.

My dear Chaos Witch, it is with great pleasure that I introduce Glycon, the Greco-Roman god of snakes. Who was also a sock puppet.

In the second century of the Common Era, a professional mystic—which is what they had in ancient Greece in place of social media influencers—named Alexander announced the pending arrival of a new incarnation of Asclepius, the god of healing and medicine. On the scheduled date of the incarnation's arrival, Alexander gathered a crowd in the marketplace of his hometown Abonoteichos, and as the sun reached its noonday peak, he pulled out a large goose egg and broke it open, revealing a snake.[53]

A week later, the serpent, dubbed Glycon, had grown to roughly five feet in length and had somehow developed a human head, complete with flowing blonde hair. Glycon could speak and issue prophecies to his devotees, and word spread that he had the ability to cure infertility.

The cult of Glycon got very popular very quickly, flowing out of Greece and into Rome, although the Roman satirist Lucian was deeply peeved by the whole thing, pointing out that while Glycon's body did seem to be that of a large, tame constrictor, his head was just a big puppet animated by Alexander. Lucian also claimed that

---

53. Regius, *Lucian vs. the False Prophet*.

Glycon's famed powers of fertility had less to do with anything miraculous, and more to do with Alexander's boundary issues.

Alexander himself shuffled off the mortal coil in 170 CE, and without its fearless leader, the cult of Glycon faded away after a century or so. However, Glycon himself was not forgotten. In fact, he's still venerated today.

In a 2003 interview with the magazine *Arthur*, comic book author and Ceremonial Magician Alan Moore spoke of his personal devotion to Glycon, stating, "If I'm gonna have a god I prefer it to be a complete hoax and a glove puppet because I'm not likely to start believing that glove puppet created the universe or anything like that."[54]

Moore went on to explain that to him, the *idea* of the god *was* the god, adding, "[M]agicians would say there was a 'serpent current,' if you like, an energy, that people could connect up to. And they might understand this energy in a number of different forms—as Asclepius, or Glycon or Kundalini or whatever—but it's essentially a kind of sinuous kind of energy that we associate with the snake and a certain sort of consciousness." In other words, Glycon represents the embodiment of a serpentine egregore. And while Glycon himself may have just been a pet snake with his head stuck in an oversized mask, his likeness can be utilized to tap into a greater archetype.

To sum up, Glycon was (and is) a pop culture deity. And if he can still be venerated today, so too can any number of egregores and personifications, all patiently waiting for you to decide they exist.

---

54. Babcock, "Magic Is Afoot."

Putting the Cult in Popular Culture

A standard reaction to the thought of pop culture occultism is, "Well, *somebody's* been dabbling in one too many role-playing games…" But the metaphysical has always drawn inspiration from fiction, and there is a lot of power to be found in that.

In *Condensed Chaos*, Phil Hine offers the following point of view:

"One aspect of Chaos Magick that seems to upset some people is the Chaos Magician's (or Chaoist, if you like) occasional fondness for working with images culled from non-historical sources, such as invoking H. P Lovecraft's Cthulhu Mythos beings, mapping the Rocky Horror Show onto the Tree of Life, slamming through the astral void in an X-Wing fighter, and 'channeling' communications from gods that didn't exist five minutes ago."[55]

Hine also talks about getting "interesting results" from rituals based on C. S. Lewis's *Chronicles of Narnia*, a series of novels based on Christian theology. In Greater Pagandom, the venerable Church of All Worlds was inspired by the science fiction novel *Stranger in a Strange Land*; back in the 1990s, Klingon Wicca was an actual thing; and in 2015, the Temple of the Jedi Order was granted IRS tax exemption as a religious organization. My own beliefs were profoundly influenced by the novel *Kraken* and the stage play *A Perfect Ganesh*, but they were also deeply affected by *Skinny Legs and All* by Tom Robbins and *The King Must Die* by Mary Renault.

Even the myths that we treasure are just stories that some ancient person conceived and/or wrote down at some point. They're amazing and useful and educational to be sure…but they're just stories. No matter how heavily we rely on them.

---

55. Hine, *Condensed Chaos*, 139.

But that doesn't mean they're not true. Nor does it mean that the characters who appear in those stories can't be brought into the real world (whatever that is).

From an esoteric standpoint, fictional characters can evolve into egregores—spirit-like entities residing in Kia and manifesting in Aether, who come into existence through collective belief. When a comic superhero or the protagonist of a book series gains traction with readers and starts growing in popularity, their personality traits and attributes become canon, and that character can take on an independent life of its own.

Not to get overly meta here, but *American Gods* by Neil Gaiman provides excellent examples of egregores in action. Within the novel, the gods and spirits of the Old World are brought to the New World as people migrate from the former to the latter. But over time, people stop believing as much in their gods, and so those gods have to get jobs. Meanwhile, new gods start spawning as secular faith shifts away from religion and toward industrialization: gods like Technology, Media, and Conspiracy Theory. These new gods are egregores—they came into existence once enough people believed in them.

And here's an even better example. After winning an academy award for her portrayal of Clarice Starling in *The Silence of the Lambs*, Jodie Foster famously turned down the opportunity to reprise the role in *Hannibal*. Officially, Foster cited scheduling conflicts, but she also claimed that she didn't want to "trample" Starling, indicating that she wasn't comfortable with how the character was depicted in the sequel.[56] The author Thomas Harris may have invented the character Clarice Starling for a novel, but Foster *knew* Starling; she'd spent a big chunk of time *as* Starling; and she

---

56. "The Total Film Interview—Jodie Foster."

had a deep understanding of how Starling would have reacted true to form when dropped into the events of *Hannibal*.

Whether consciously or not, Foster channeled Starling as an egregore. So take some time to think about the egregores you know well, and how they can be of assistance to you. And if one seems to provide more consistent prompt succor than any other—say, Scrooge McDuck consistently comes through and helps you save money—there is nothing preventing you from doing what Mal-2 and Lord Omar did and starting your own religion.

Let's figure out how to do that.

The All-Seeing Eye of the Storm

Since I've already fanboyed extensively over the Scarlet Witch, I'm going to turn to another Marvel heroine around which to build a devotion: Ororo Munroe, better known as Storm of the X-Men.

When she was first introduced to readers back in 1975, Storm believed herself to be a goddess. In fact, her arrival is heralded by a group of villagers summoning her through song, "Ororo, great goddess of the storm, come unto us and ease our burden."[57]

Right away, we've got an invocation, which clearly works, because Ororo answers the call. The villagers offer to sacrifice ten goats and chickens to her if Ororo will bring rain to end the drought, to which she replies, "Save your beasts, my children. You need them more than I. I will do as you plead." So we also know that physical offerings are not necessary when venerating Ororo, although praise does seem to be an effective oblation.

Ororo eventually assumed leadership of the X-Men, and she took command of the underground community of mutants known as the Morlocks after a fight to the (almost) death with

---
57. Wein and Cockrum, *Giant-Size X-Men #1*.

their previous ruler. While she abhors the taking of life, she is not afraid to kill in the line of duty, so in addition to being a storm goddess, we can also see her as a goddess of war, strategy, and sovereignty—especially after she married T'Challa, the Black Panther, and became queen of Wakanda. And speaking of, Ororo has had several long-term romantic relationships, both with men and at least one woman, so we can perceive her as a goddess of love as well. Plus, she's an accomplished thief, making her the patroness of those who operate outside the law.

You know, Ororo is starting to sound a lot like Astarte, Ishtar, and Inanna. In fact, the period in the comics when Ororo's powers were taken away from her could be read as a modern retelling of the Descent of Inanna. But here's the best part: For much of her tenure with the X-Men, Ororo wore a distinctive tiara, the design of which has become an unmistakable emblem. What this means for us is that Ororo comes with her very own sigil, which you can make use of when venerating her.

Because of her equation with Inanna, Ororo is associated with the planet Venus, which means Friday would be the appropriate day of the week to pray to her. And when she first joined the X-Men, she turned down a bedroom in the X-Mansion, preferring instead to move into an attic, which she filled with flowering plants. As such, her altars should always have live flowers on them.

Crafting with Chaos
Cutting Cords

Whether we want them to or not, relationships sometimes come to an end. This can be true of interpersonal connections in the real world as well as a partnership fostered with a particular deity. In either case, a time may come to cut ties and move on.

The pictures and videos of cord-cutting spells I've seen online usually involve two taper candles set a few inches apart and connected by a piece of string. The idea is that as the candles burn down, the string will eventually alight and burn away, and the spell will be complete. It's a workable setup, but honestly, I have a couple of concerns with it.

First off, it's the fire hazard to end all fire hazards, and second, it's unpredictable. The string might catch fire, or it might get stuck in the wax, or it might just droop and slide down as the candles melt. But if you're determined to use this method, awkward calls to your insurance adjuster be damned, the following spell is less incendiary.

You will need

Two matching taper candles (white or the color you associate with Bureaucracy)

A knife

String or twine, at least ten inches in length

Two candleholders

A pair of scissors

Directions

Starting at the base and working toward the wick, use the knife to carve your name vertically into one of the candles. Carve the other person's name vertically into the second candle, but this time start at the wick and move toward the base. Take a length of string, tie one end around the middle of your candle, and the other end around the middle of the other person's candle. Set the candles in the holders a few inches apart.

Light the other person's candle first and let it burn for five minutes. *Do not leave it unattended.* Then light your candle. After doing so, grab your scissors and recite the following:

Fate has bound [name of other person] to me, but I take Fate into my hands. By the powers of the Morai, personifications of Fate, I cut the cord that connects us.

Snip through the string and let the candles burn down.

Don't let chance determine whether or not the cord is cut. Make the conscious decision to cut it yourself.

All this said, the first rule of casting a cord-cutting spell is, don't tell everyone on social media that you're casting a cord-cutting spell. Seriously. If you're truly trying to make a clean break from someone, talking about them and posting pictures of the work you're doing just reinforces that connection instead of severing it. Keeping the work to yourself until after it's accomplished will get you much better results than dragging your friends and followers along with you.

And while we're on the subject of social media: If you're casting a cord-cutting spell, but you're still connected to the other person on various platforms, you're not truly cutting anything. Block them. Or unfollow them, or unfriend them, or all of the above. Making a show of cutting magical ties while leaving digital ties in place is disingenuous. If you're going to cut cords, cut *all* of them.

As discussed in chapter 5, your spells will produce the best effects when you can cast them without worrying about them—when your determination is stronger than your emotional investment. Following this logic, cord-cutting spells will only work when you are fully ready to let go of a given person, place, or thing, and you are able to walk away with the knowledge that you are finally free.

Chapter 9

Ethical Chaos and the Curse of Greyface

As a Chaos Witch, your personal ethics will ultimately derive from whichever belief system you happen to be exploring: If your current beliefs revolve around nontheistic Satanism, you'll probably be living by the Seven Fundamental Tenets; if your beliefs involve Heathenism, you'll want to uphold the Aesirian Code of Nine. But the broader concepts of right and wrong vary from paradigm to paradigm. The Chaos trick is to not let yourself be wedded to or bogged down by any of them, while still putting them to use in your Witchcraft.

The phrase *nothing is true, everything is permitted* is bandied about quite a bit in Chaos-oriented spaces. And while it's a pretty clear statement on paper, the deeper meaning is sometimes debated, mainly because people outside of the Chaos current (and sometimes people within it) take it to mean that any belief or practice is up for grabs as a tool, regardless of where it may or may not have originated, or which culture it ultimately belongs to. In other words, "Chaos Witchcraft means that I can do whatever I want, without consequence." But we have to remember that every action will *always* have some kind of reaction.

I am legally allowed to consume alcohol, but I'm also a recovering alcoholic, and I know what happens when I put alcohol in my body, so I choose not to do that. And yes, nothing may be true, and everything may be permitted, but we also need to keep in mind what we learned from Jeff Goldblum in *Jurassic Park* (1993)—playing a mathematician who specializes in Chaos Theory, coincidentally enough: *Just because we can doesn't mean we should.*

Army of Popes

In Discordianism, everyone is a Pope. Literally everyone. If you're reading this, you are a Pope; if someone is reading this over your shoulder, they're a Pope too. As it says in the *Principia*, "A Pope is someone who is not under the authority of the authorities," which means that as a Discordian, you have complete power over your actions, beliefs, and morality.[58] No one can tell you what to do or think except you.

One of the fringe benefits of being a Pope is that you get to carry a cunning Pope Card, the original of which can be found within the *Principia Discordia*. Traditionally, Discordians would photocopy that page and cut out the card to keep in their wallets, but today, you can find the template online and print out your own. (You can also write to me, and I will send you one for free.)

Papal infallibility aside, the only behavioral rules to which Discordians are encouraged to adhere are those set out in the Five Commandments provided by the Apostle Zarathud, which are collectively known as the Pentabarf. The kicker is that the com-

---
58. Hill and Thornley, *Principia Discordia*, 00036.

mandments can't really be followed, since they tend to contradict themselves and cancel each other out.

> **THE BEARER OF THIS CARD IS A GENUINE AND AUTHORIZED**
>
>
>
> So *please* Treat Them Right
>
> **GOOD FOREVER**
>
> Genuine and authorized by the HOUSE of ERIS
>
> ---
>
> Every individual on this Earth is a genuine and authorized Pope.
> Reproduce and distribute these cards freely
> P.O.E.E Head Temple, San Francisco

Discordian Pope Card

Here is the Pentabarf as it is presented in the *Principia*:

I—There is no Goddess but Goddess and She is Your Goddess. There is no Erisian Movement but The Erisian Movement and it is The Erisian Movement. And every Golden Apple Corps is the beloved home of a Golden Worm.

II—A Discordian Shall Always use the Official Discordian Document Numbering System.

III—A Discordian is Required during his early Illumination to Go Off Alone & Partake Joyously of a Hot Dog on a Friday; this Devotive Ceremony to Remonstrate against the popular Paganisms of the Day: of Catholic Christendom (no meat on Friday), of Judaism (no meat of Pork), of Hindic Peoples (no meat of Beef), of Buddhists (no meat of animal), and of Discordians (no Hot Dog Buns).

IV—A Discordian shall Partake of No Hot Dog Buns, for Such was the Solace of Our Goddess when She was Confronted with The Original Snub.

V—A Discordian is Prohibited of Believing what he reads.[59]

On the surface, the Pentabarf is a satirical send-up of the tenets of organized religion and not to be taken seriously. The Official Discordian Numbering System, for example, found on page 00020 of the *Principia*, is intentionally confounding to the point of uselessness. But it's the Fifth Commandment—the one that invalidates the other four—where a heavier meaning comes to light. As a Pope, you may not have to do what anyone else says, but you are also charged to think critically, and to not accept anything without question.

Equal and Opposite Reactions

The downside to an all-Pope religion is that unfortunately, we can't hold anyone accountable for our actions except ourselves, which also means that we have to accept the consequences of our actions. I may fully believe that monetary wealth should be equally distributed among all people, but if I decide to make that happen by robbing a bank, I am going to jail. Explaining to the judge that Eris told me to do it will not get my charges dismissed.

Mind you, "consequence" does not automatically mean getting in trouble: If I cast a Discord spell to get a coworker fired, and they get fired, no one from HR is going to toss my office for miscreant sigils. Nor is a consequence necessarily a bad thing. If I cast a Bureaucracy spell to help a friend get over a head cold, and my friend gets better, their recovery is at least partially a conse-

---

[59]. Hill and Thornley, *Principia Discordia*, 00004.

quence of my action. But as Witches, especially Chaos Witches, we do need to own both the positive and the negative results of our magic.

One of Stephen King's greatest short stories, entitled "Everything's Eventual," centers on a young man named Dinky, who has the power to control other people through sigils. King never refers to them as sigils—his protagonist can just draw shapes no one has ever seen before and can customize them by adding words and names—but they're totally sigils. Regardless, Dinky's abilities land him on the radar of a clandestine organization that recruits him as a long-range assassin.

For a long while, he's content with his life. He likes using his power, and he doesn't mind killing. However, when he learns that his targets are progressive political activists and critical thinkers with growing audiences, he makes plans to escape the organization. Assassination only becomes an ethical issue for him when he realizes that his targets are people he believes are trying to do some good in the world.

When we talk about beliefs, you might think of religion, gods, spirits, and magic, and those certainly all involve belief. But belief as an artifact is a lot wider and more nuanced than just religion and spirituality. And if we restrict our understanding of belief to just those things, we're really putting some limits on how capable we can be as Chaos Witches.

Whatever your ethics happen to be, they will come into play as you assemble the various bits and bobs of your personal Chaos practice. It's common to hear people say "I take from everything" when describing Eclectic Witchcraft, but "taking" implies a change in ownership—what once belonged to one person or group now belongs to someone else. And contrary to the opinions you may encounter on social media, when it comes to Witchcraft, not everything belongs to everyone.

So, before you do anything else with Chaos Witchcraft, it's imperative that you examine the beliefs you already hold, determine where they came from and why they are important to you, and set aside the ones that are holding you back. Starting with open and closed practices.

Aneristically Open, Eristically Closed

The botanist Frederic Clements first espoused the idea that ecological systems, unmolested, will eventually reach a steady state of self-sufficiency, and his theories made the jump from ecology to sociology in the identification of what are now called closed communities. Closed communities can be ethnic, regional, or religious in nature (or combo platters of all three), but all of them limit their interactions with outsiders, and members of closed communities are either born into them or accepted into them on an individual basis.

Examples of closed communities include the Amish, the Roma, Haitian Vodou, and Judaism. Within Paganism, initiatory Traditions are closed communities. And I don't know exactly when the one word managed to replace the other, but it's really important that we stress *community* over *practice*, because if we only focus on cherry-picked parts of closed systems, we leave way too much room for reinforced marginalization.

When determining whether a given practice is open or closed, start at the tip of a pyramid and work your way down: Cartomancy? Open. Ritual cartomancy? Open. Ritual cartomancy in the Romani tradition? Closed. It's only when a specific practice is nestled within the context of a given community that the door swings shut, not before.

And while working on determining what is open and closed, pay special attention to what members of those communities have to say on the matter, because a big part of the issue with the non-marginalized understanding of closed practices has to do with how we're defining *practice*. On multiple occasions, I've heard someone say, "Peyote is a closed practice," or, "Chakras are a closed practice," or, "Tarot is a closed practice." But peyote is a *plant*; the ritual use of peyote within an Indigenous religious ceremony is a *practice*.

Another example: chakras are energy points that correspond to collections of nerve bundles in the human body. An exercise designed to open a particular chakra in a Buddhist or Hindu context is a practice, but the chakras themselves just conceptually exist, regardless of whether or not we acknowledge or poke at them.

The tarot is a deck of playing cards that originated in Italy and was eventually repurposed as a method of divination in eighteenth-century France. The unique set of techniques for reading tarot passed down within Romani culture is a practice.

It's a linguistic issue more than anything else, but it's a symptom of a larger problem. Many of us in the global minority don't have firsthand lived experience within a closed culture, so we're not always able to accurately identify what artifacts are or are not readily available to us. Terms like *open practice* and *closed practice* can be helpful, but because we've allowed dominant groups to have the final say on what is open or closed, with little or no input from marginalized groups, those labels have become arbitrary and are in danger of becoming meaningless.

with spirits. Divination and what we now call demonolatry would fall under the dreadful header of black magic.[62]

And then the Protestant Reformation happened, and suddenly, it was *all* black magic; it was *all* witchcraft and devil worship. And that was pretty much the standard screed, right up until Victorian times, when a romanticized interest in Paganism started developing. But it was also during this time that *black magic* took on racial connotations. The term started being applied to the religious and magical practices of non-European cultures, particularly those in Haiti and the South Seas. When viewed through a European cultural grid, these practices were seen as exotic, dangerous, and evil, a perception that was reinforced by Hollywood, beginning in the 1920s and continuing today. The 1932 film *White Zombie*, for instance, set in Haiti, pits "heroes" of European descent against the powerful "African superstitions" of a sinister voodoo master.[63] It's worth noting that the voodoo master is also of European descent, and he's the villain because he was "corrupted" by practicing African magic.

The term *white magic*, on the other hand, really didn't work its way into common vernacular until the 1960s and '70s, when there was a concerted push to differentiate between Pagan witchcraft and Satanism, and the term remained in use in the 1980s and '90s, in defense against the ongoing Satanic Panic.

And then, in the early 2000s, Pagans of European descent "discovered" Hoodoo, and they started gobbling up Crossing rituals, and Hot Foot Powder, and sour jars, and Death unto My Enemy spells without attribution—hexing and cursing techniques that, at the time,

---

62. Summers, *Witchcraft and Black Magic*, 19-42.

63. Greene, *Lights, Camera, Witchcraft*, 83.

Discordian Dance Break

Baneful Magic

Within the occult, the word *baneful* was originally used in reference to dangerous plants. Like, poisonous herbs that were hazardous to work with: *Those were baneful*.[60] It's really only been since the early 2020s that *baneful* has been applied to broader magical practice. And in the grand scheme of things, that's okay—there have always been and always will be influxes of new ideas into European-based witchcraft: Baneful magic, trickster spirits, return-to-sender spells, cord-cutting spells, lemon hexes, and moon water are all examples of either brand-new ideas or less-new ideas that have been reworked and repurposed. This does not mean that they are not useful, or that they are not valid.

That said, Witches started saying *baneful magic* to avoid the bias and negative connotations inherent in the phrase *black magic*. However, racial bias is very much still present in baneful magic—we've just given it a new name.

Way back in the age of the fifteenth-century grimoire traditions, there was no distinction between black magic and white magic. Instead, there was a distinction between black magic and *natural magic*.[61] Natural magic toed the line of science and included subjects like astrology, alchemy, and herbalism, along with any ritual practices that were supposed to bring one closer to the Christian god. Black magic, on the other hand, was consorting

---

60. Michael, *The Poison Path Herbal*, 1.
61. Agrippa, *The Fourth Book of Occult Philosophy*, 9–10.

were not covered by the popular Pagan books. All these co-opted Hoodoo practices remain in Witchcraft today, but they have been rebranded as baneful magic.

If witches describe their practices as *baneful* magic instead of *black* magic to avoid racist connotations, and yet they are referring to African American folk magic as baneful because it's exotic and dangerous, a racial bias is still being upheld—we're just calling it something different to draw attention away from that.

Instead of categorizing hexes and curses under the special heading of baneful, consider just calling them hexes and curses. From a Chaos Witchcraft perspective, magic is magic—any differentiation between good and bad is irrelevant and unnecessary.

Chaos and Appropriation

While I normally rail against binaries, I do suspect that there are two types of Witches in the world: Those who saw *Bring It On* (2000) at an impressionable age, and those who did not. If you haven't had a chance to watch this film yourself, here's a synopsis.

The Rancho Carne Toros are a five-time national champion cheerleading squad from an affluent suburb outside of Los Angeles, and when the main character, Torrance, takes the helm as team captain, she discovers that all of her team's award-winning routines had been stolen from the East Compton Clovers—a cheerleading squad from an inner city school. Torrance makes several attempts to set things right, all of which blow up in her face, and finally, the Toros decide to just come up with a brand-new routine. And they do so, as per the script, by studying other forms of movement and drawing inspiration from them, thus creating something that no one had ever seen before. And they end up having a spectacular showing at nationals, coming in second place to the Clovers.

From a cultural standpoint, the Toros started out the movie engaging in appropriation, which occurs whenever a given practice (or tradition, or fashion) that originates within a marginalized group is adopted by the members of a dominant group, resulting in one or more of the following outcomes:

- The dominant group does not credit the marginalized group for originating the practice.
- The dominant group denies the marginalized group access to practice.
- The dominant group refuses to compensate the marginalized group while actively profiting off the practice.
- The dominant group condemns the marginalized group for continuing to engage in the practice.

Let's look at a couple of scenarios to make sure we understand what cultural appropriation is. In the first scenario, you decide to make a burrito. You get a tortilla, fill it with meat, beans, and cheese, and just to see how it tastes, you add some Sriracha and crushed potato chips. Then you eat it.

Is this cultural appropriation?

No. This is lunch, consumed in the privacy of your own home, for nobody's benefit but your own. It is not a traditional meal by any means, but you are also not attempting to capitalize on it, nor pass your culinary experiment off as authentic Mexican food.

In the second scenario, you open a food cart specializing in burritos and quickly achieve some renown for your delicious handmade tortillas. You end up spotlighted by a local news outlet, and during the interview, you explain that although you are not from Mexico nor of Mexican descent, you recently vacationed there, and you just fell in love with the tortillas—however, no one would teach you how to make them. In response, you snuck around and peeked in kitchen windows and spied on cooks until you figured out the proper techniques and ingredients. Then you went home and launched a business selling "authentic" Mexican food.

Is this cultural appropriation?

Absolutely, and it actually happened in Portland back in 2017, a city where people of color were having to jump through a crushing number of hoops to open food carts, only to be routinely denied permits. Meanwhile, white Portlandians were not encountering the same obstacles, nor were they subjected to inordinate fines for not having the proper permits. And this included two women of European descent, who were running a burrito cart and went on the evening news to brag about stealing recipes.[64]

So why, in this day and age, do things like this keep occurring, both in the mundane and the occult worlds? Why are closed practices still perceived as up for grabs? Why do some Pagans continue to misdirect away from their own appropriative behaviors by blaming everything on Wicca?

The answer—or at least the Discordian answer—is painfully simple: It's all because Greyface says so.

The Adversarial Archenemy You Didn't Know You Needed to Know

Greyface is the personification of the Protestant-based, capitalistic culture in which we reside. If the Apostles of Eris—Hung Mung, Dr. Van Van Mojo, Sri Syadasti, Zarathud, and the Elder Malaclypse—are the avatars of Creative Disorder, Greyface is the avatar of Destructive Order.

Page 00042 of the *Principia Discordia* describes Greyface with uncharacteristically somber words: "In the year 1166 B.C., a malcontented hunchbrain by the name of Greyface, got it into his head that the universe was as humorless as he, and he began to teach that play was sinful because it contradicted the ways of Serious Order."

The year 1166 BC(E) is an interesting choice for the emergence of Greyface. I assume that Mal-2 and Lord Omar picked that date because the digits add up to five (1+1+6+6=14; 1+4=5). However, contemporary research indicates that the Late Bronze Age collapsed around 1177 BCE, so whether they meant to be historically

---

64. Moreno, "Portland Burrito Cart Closes After Owners Are Accused of Cultural Appropriation."

accurate or not, by their reckoning, Greyface showed up right at the dawn of the Iron Age.[65]

Inexplicably, Greyface attracted followers who devoted themselves to him and his oppressive beliefs unconditionally, going so far as to destroy anyone who disagreed with them, or whose way of life in any way deviated from their own. By teaching that the Aneristic Illusion was in fact reality and by encouraging his followers to disregard Creation and Destruction as the only true polarity in favor of the artificial concepts of Order and Disorder, Greyface introduced binary thinking into the world. And by holding up Order as more correct than Disorder, he forced the cultures around him to live oppressed under Destructive Order, with no opportunity to reclaim the freedom of Creative Disorder. As described by the *Principia*: "The unfortunate result of this is that mankind has since been suffering from a psychological and spiritual imbalance. Imbalance causes frustration, and frustration causes fear. And fear makes for a bad trip. Man has been on a bad trip for a long time now."[66]

The Curse of Greyface enforces comparisons; it tells us that something can only be good if something else is bad, or that for something to achieve validity, it has to be inherently better than something else. Rooted firmly in the Protestant Christian ethics that influence all aspects of our society (whether we realize it or not), the Curse of Greyface demands that scapegoats and sin-eaters—individuals and groups deemed lesser than—take the blame for any problems we encounter, while the true sources of those problems remain safely in the shadows.

---

65. Cline and Fawkes, *1177 B.C.*
66. Hill and Thornley, *Principia Discordia*, 00042.

The Curse of Greyface makes us rigid, not just in our religious beliefs, but in our perceptions of outside spiritualities, which only exist to be strip-mined and persecuted. It pits polarities against each other and breeds entitlement. It teaches us that fads are more important than sustainability; and, most detrimentally, it keeps us too distracted with infighting and competition to pay attention to real-world plights that could quite literally be the death of us all.

Think of how polarized the political landscape of the United States became in the late 2010s and early 2020s, when marginalized groups were scapegoated by extremist candidates to gaslight their constituents into an Us vs. Them mentality. Outside of politics, we can look at what happened to Twitter for another real-time analogy of Greyface in action.

Up until 2022, the social media platform formerly known as Twitter was a lawless but joyful place. And then Elon Musk decided that he wanted it all for himself and purchased it for forty-four billion dollars, dictating new restrictions on users while firing engineers who had managed for years to somehow keep the platform running. Most worthy of cringe, he removed verifications. No longer would celebrities and world leaders have a blue checkmark on their accounts to designate that they were in fact who they said they were—instead, anyone could obtain a blue checkmark by becoming a paid monthly subscriber.

At that moment, Musk was acting as a lackey of Greyface, and he foisted Destructive Order upon the Creative Disorder that was Twitter. And as we know from the Law of Eristic Escalation, whenever Destructive Order is imposed on Creative Disorder, Destructive Disorder results. Advertisers pulled their marketing and went off to find other social media demographics, and users left in droves. Twitter still exists as of this writing (we're supposed to call it X now), but it's a bombed-out shell of what it once was.

Gninoitidnoced

Fortunately, as Chaos Witches, we have the resources to fight back against the agents of Destructive Disorder in the world. We just have to make the internal decision—one might even call it an ethical choice—to embrace the Creative over the Destructive. Just as dialectical behavioral therapy is utilized to help patients with emotional challenges understand that more than one concept can be true at the same time, Discordianism encourages us to accept that as synthetic structures, Order and Disorder are equals, not opponents.

This is where the Principle of Deconditioning comes fully into play. Those of us raised in a Greyface culture are used to passively listening to him, of automatically thinking in terms of good and bad, or right and wrong. If you're going to make any kind of difference as a practitioner of Chaos Witchcraft, it is crucial that you actively attempt to disentangle yourself from the sticky web of Greyface's lies and manipulations.

In *Mastering Witchcraft*, author Paul Huson presents a ritual of unbinding, which includes reading the Lord's Prayer backward on three consecutive nights.[67] He also provides a phonetic transliteration, as follows:

Nema!
Livee morf su revilled tub
Noishaytpmet ootni ton suh deel
Suh tshaiga sapsert tath yeth
Vigrawf eu za sesapsert rua suh vigrawf.
Derb ilaid rua yed sith suh vig

---

[67]. Huson, *Mastering Witchcraft*, 9.

Neveh ni si za thre ni
Nud eeb liw eyth
Muck mod-ngik eyth
Main eyth eeb dwohlah
Neveh ni tra chioo
Rertharf rua!

Author Sarah Lyons also encourages the initiatory breaking of taboos in *Revolutionary Witchcraft*, along with crafting chain links out of construction paper and ritually tearing free of them. The point of these rituals is not to blaspheme, but to decondition; to unshackle yourself from the hold that the Curse of Greyface has over our culture. And the more you decondition, the more capable you are of launching a few curses of your own.

Gobble, Gobble, Foil and Hobble

As mentioned previously, the Turkey Curse was devised by the Apostle Dr. Van Van Mojo, with the expressed purpose of disrupting the Aneristic intentions of Greyface and his lackeys. To throw the curse, square off against your target and assume the stance of an old-timey boxer. Once you have their attention, begin waving your arms about mystically, take a deep breath, and gobble five times like a turkey as loudly as you can. At which point your foe will get weirded out and leave you alone.

The Turkey Curse can be performed as written, but it can also be understood as a general metaphor for injecting Creative Disorder into otherwise Destructively Ordered situations. If you find yourself squaring off against a troll on social media, try responding to their insults with polite but completely noncontextual comments: "My apologies, but I'm no longer the sausage king of

Chicago," or my go-to, "What a coincidence! That was my nickname in prison." Speaking from personal experience, I can say that the troll will inevitably be too baffled to continue the conversation. You could also purchase a blue checkmark on Twitter, impersonate pharmaceutical giant Eli Lilly, and announce to the world that insulin is now free—another thing that actually happened.[68]

When Musk did away with Twitter's verification process, users did in fact pay money for those coveted blue checkmarks. However, they then utilized their newfound online clout to create parody accounts, putting truly unhinged statements in the mouths of celebrities, politicians, and big businesses, to amazing effect. In the previous case, Eli Lilly was forced to publicly admit that insulin was not actually free—an announcement which caused their stock to plummet. To amend the ensuing PR disaster, the out-of-pocket cost of insulin was capped at thirty-five dollars, making it actually affordable to those who needed it to survive.

This is the kind of benevolent impact that the lunacy of the Turkey Curse can have in our Aneristic world. Regardless of your personal ethics, as a Chaos Witch, your higher calling is the magical application of Creative Disorder.

Crafting with Chaos
The Pringles® Can Curse

The Pringles® Can Curse was originally devised by social media omni-lord Riot Addams, and it is reprinted here with his permission along with a couple of tweaks by me, based on Discordianism and personal preference.

---

68. Pintado, "'Twitter Blue Parody Accounts Flood the Platform After New Subscription Service Rollout."

You will need

A stick of incense

An empty can of Pringles® with some crumbs at the bottom (Riot suggests Sour Cream and Onion, although I'd go with Salt and Vinegar)

A handful of dirt (just regular dirt, although graveyard dirt would also work well)

Kallisti Powder (recipe follows the directions)

A packet of hot sauce

Cigarette butts (or any other gross trash)

A bottle of nighttime liquid cold medicine

Broken glass or nails

Paper and pen

A full cup of water (moon or otherwise)

Duct tape

A votive candle (of the color of your choice)

Directions

Light the incense and cense the can, inside and out. Pour the dirt in the can, to bury your enemy. Add the Kallisti Powder, then squeeze the hot sauce into the can and drop the empty packet in as well. Add the butts or the trash (because they're garbage), then pour in a good swig of the cold medicine (to put them to sleep). Add the broken glass or nails, then write your target's name on a slip of paper, fold it five times—always folding away from you—then set it on fire, and drop it into the can. Follow this immediately with the water.

Once you've confirmed that the paper fire is out, put the lid back on the can and seal it shut with the duct tape, as Riot says, "Like it's the coffin our enemies will be resting in." Set the candle on top of the can. Once it's burned all the way down (the candle, that is, not the entire can), dispose of the spell remains far away from your home.

Whether or not you actually cast the Pringles® Can Curse is entirely up to you and your own personal ethics. If hexing or cursing isn't your thing, I promise that's fine: You are absolutely not required to curse anyone or anything if it conflicts with your personal moral code, or even if you just don't feel like doing it.

And if you're *really into* hexing and cursing, I promise that's fine as well. Whatever magical work you do, "baneful" or not, is strictly between you and your gods. If they're cool with it, then I'm cool with it too.

Recipe for Kallisti Powder

Adding Kallisti Powder to a hex or curse is the Chaos Witchcraft equivalent of tossing a golden apple into a wedding banquet. It is a blend of the following:

1 part black mustard seeds

1 part ground patchouli leaves

1 part poppy seeds

1 part red pepper flakes

5–23 parts gold glitter (measure with your heart)

Chapter 10
Chaos Spirituality

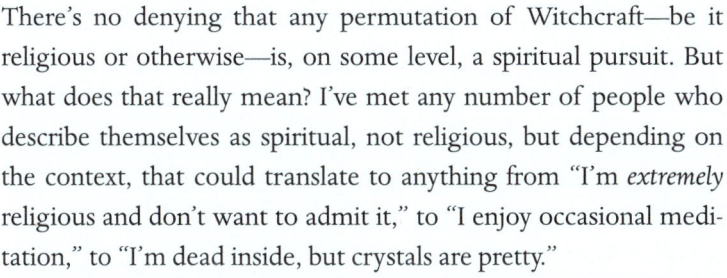

There's no denying that any permutation of Witchcraft—be it religious or otherwise—is, on some level, a spiritual pursuit. But what does that really mean? I've met any number of people who describe themselves as spiritual, not religious, but depending on the context, that could translate to anything from "I'm *extremely* religious and don't want to admit it," to "I enjoy occasional meditation," to "I'm dead inside, but crystals are pretty."

Within 12-step programs, recovering addicts and alcoholics talk about spirituality a *lot*, and when I first got sober, I found myself stymied by that. I mean, I got that God (singular or plural) was somehow involved, but I couldn't help noticing that everyone kept saying "spiritual" without offering any insight into what they meant by that.

Let's take some time to deconstruct the notion of spirituality, and how it applies to the framework of Chaos Witchcraft. It won't be an easy process, but there will be moments of fun and silliness to balance out any potential discomfort.

And to get the ball rolling, let's turn to the *Principia Discordia* for some direction.

Brother in Spirit

At some point after the universe was up and running, Void found himself vaguely dissatisfied. He'd made Eris and Aneris, who were keeping themselves busy creating and destroying things, but all their machinations were *physical* in nature. There was nothing *metaphysical* going on; no soul to gain awareness of all the Chaos, much less enjoy it.

Void decided to take some time off and sort this out, so he locked himself in his Void cave for five eras. And when he emerged, Eris and Aneris were startled to discover that he'd given birth to another child: Spirituality—whom, the *Principia* points out, had no name at all.[69]

Eris and Aneris were pretty uncomfortable with the whole affair—not because their dad was once again spontaneously shooting out babies like a seahorse, but because of a shared worry that Void would give all his attention to the new kid.

"My girls, you have nothing to worry about," Void assured them. "I love all my children equally. And to prove it, we're going to co-parent!"

Eris and Aneris were skeptical.

"No, really," Void said. It's going to be great. Since he has no form, Spirituality will start out living with Aneris in a state of Non-Being. But then he'll get to go live with Eris in a state of Being."

---

69. Hill and Thornley, *Principia Discordia*, 00057.

"Wait a second," Eris said. "Aneris destroys everything I create. Once Spirituality comes to live with me, Aneris will destroy him too."

"Oh, yeah," Aneris said, popping a handful of freshly minted planetoids in her mouth and munching away. "I totally will."

"Okay... good point," Void said. "So how about this: Spirituality will live with Aneris, then live with Eris, and after that, he'll come back and stay with me."

Which leads us to a line from the *Principia* that never fails to give me goose bumps: "And so it is that we, as men, do not exist until we do; and then it is that we play with our world of existent things, and order and disorder them, and so it shall be that non-existence shall take us back from existence and that nameless spirituality shall return to Void, like a tired child home from a very wild circus."[70]

Spirituality is, at least in part, the sentience of the human experience: From nonexistence we were created, and, after the series of wacky misadventures that is life, to the void we shall return. And I really like this definition, because it clears away some of the vagueness around the idea, and it gives us something to consider.

Eventually, I found another, more concrete definition that worked well for me, and that I think will work well for you too.

Spirituality is the process of becoming who we're supposed to be.

Alcohol prevented me from being myself, so as part of the spiritual process, I cut it out of my life. Witchcraft is an inherent part of who I am, so pursuing it is also part of the spiritual process. Discordianism grants me a profound sense of where I've been and where I'm going, so it's a huge part of the spiritual process. Spirituality is

---

70. Hill and Thornley, *Principia Discordia*, 00058.

sentience, but as sentient beings, we have the chance to figure out where our potential lies, and how to go about unlocking and achieving it. That, my friends, is our spiritual journey.

Another Fruitful Wedding

The *Principia* asserts that Spirituality has no name, but Greek mythology suggests otherwise. Iasion (pronounced *Aision*), the legendary founder of the Samothracian Mysteries, was described as the brother of Harmonia (Aneris), which, in a Discordian worldview, would make him the brother of Eris and therefore a human incarnation of Spirituality.

As the story goes, Iasion was a guest at the wedding of Harmonia and the hero Cadmus, but he was lured away by Demeter to "lie in a thrice-plowed field," which is my new favorite euphemism for anything NC-17. Zeus was also at the wedding, and, consumed with jealousy (read: hypocrisy) when he learned of Demeter's tryst, killed Iasion with a lightning bolt.

What we have, then, is Iasion moving from a state of Non-Being (a non-player character at Harmonia's wedding) to a state of Being (thrice-plowed field), and then returning to Void (obliteration via Zeus). It's hardcore Discordianism cleverly disguised as a classical myth, and I for one am pleased by that.

Of course, if you don't want to identify Iasion with Spirituality, that's cool. It's also cool if you don't want to slap a name on any aspect of the Divine, or if you'd rather just focus on becoming yourself.

That just means you're spiritual, not religious. And as it turns out, there is nothing wrong with that. It's actually a really good place to start.

Send In the Clown Witches

Above all else, as a Chaos Witch, you should be enjoying your magical practice. As Phil Hine wrote in his book *Condensed Chaos*, "Magic is fun—otherwise, why do it?"[71] Fun is, in and of itself, a spiritual pursuit.

In *Lights, Camera, Witchcraft: A Critical History of Witches in American Film and Television*, author Heather Greene identifies numerous archetypes present among big- and small-screen Witches, including the Accused Woman, the Wild Child, the Vamp, the Folk Witch, the Halloween Witch, the Fantasy Crone, the Magical Mom, and the Good Fairy. Most of these are easily recognizable—picture the characters in your favorite Witch movie, and you'll be able to match them up with at least one.

But of all the archetypes Greene coins, the one that jumped out at me the most, and the one that is most relevant to the spirituality of Chaos Witchcraft, is the Clown Witch.

According to Greene, one of the earliest appearances of the Clown Witch is Momba, the Wicked Witch in the 1910 film *The Wonderful Wizard of Oz*. Momba's costume contains distinctive Victorian clown motifs, such as an oversized collar, poofy sleeves, and a pointy hat, which suggest that while she's the Big Bad of the movie, her job is to entertain rather than frighten. Greene also points to Mother Goose as a good example of the Victorian Clown Witch aesthetic.

From a storytelling standpoint, Clown Witches are not evil. But they are mischievous, and they act as foils to the protagonists—in other words, they are agents of Creative Disorder. Endora from *Bewitched* and Aunt Queenie from *Bell Book and Candle* are Clown

---
71. Hine, *Condensed Chaos*, 12.

Witches, down to their flamboyant clothes and curly red hair, which, Greene notes, is reminiscent of iconic clown wigs.

While she's not explicitly mentioned as such in *Lights, Camera, Witchcraft*, Hilda Spellman from *The Chilling Adventures of Sabrina* is an amazing Clown Witch. She's technically more of a Halloween Witch and a Magical Mom, but she was also the funniest person on the show, and she often thwarted the plans of the characters with nefarious agendas, disrupting Destructive Order with her own take on the Turkey Curse. The scene in the fifth episode of the second season (released on April 5, 2019) in which she assassinated her sister's rival via almond cookies full of arsenic is a prime example.

When it comes to their spiritual development, Clown Witches embrace who they are, and they either play by their own rules, or they make up the rules as they go along. Uncle Arthur from *Bewitched* teleports into the Stevens's living room whenever he feels like it; Double Trouble from *She-Ra and the Princesses of Power* is more concerned about giving a good performance than whether or not they're on the side of good or evil. Often queer coded and always extraordinary, Clown Witches are emancipated and, much like Phil Hine, exist to remind us that magic should be fun.

Indigenous Lakota and Dakota cultures have the *heyoka*, or sacred clown, and Western European history gives us satyr plays, court jesters, and the Lord of Misrule, all of which serve to parody social mores. However, the Clown Witch operates outside of them. Spiritually, they become who they're supposed to be by refusing to let anyone else make that decision for them. Turning to the *Principia*, we find the following:

> Magicians, especially since the Gnostic and the Quabala influences, have sought higher consciousness through

assimilation and control of universal opposites—good/evil, positive/negative, male/female, etc. But due to the steadfast pomposity of ritualism inherited from the ancient methods of the shaman, occultists have been blinded to what is perhaps the two most important pairs of apparent or earth-plane opposites: ORDER/DISORDER and SERIOUS/HUMOROUS.

This is an essential challenge to the basic concepts of all western occult thought, and [the Paratheo-Anametamystikhood Of Eris Esoteric] is humbly pleased to offer the first breakthrough in occultism since Solomon.[72]

If we take the *Principia* as a clowning manual (and why wouldn't we?), we can glean that the Clown Witch's role is to actively use magic fueled with humor to generate more humor. Ergo, the creation and spreading of humor—especially humor that helps others laugh at and accept themselves—is a spiritual pursuit.

There are a lot of examples of Clown Witches to be found outside of American cinema and television, the two stuck in my childhood memories being Witchiepoo from *H. R. Pufnstuf* and Benita Bizarre from *The Bugaloos*. And they are awesome, but when you're looking for Clown Witches to exemplify on your spiritual journey, you'll want to narrow down the list to those who have the qualities you most want to embody.

You'll want to focus on the Clown Witches who are self-possessed and able to do whatever they please, all while entertaining anyone around them with irreverence and a little light blasphemy—the Sisters of Perpetual Indulgence, an order of drag nuns founded in San Francisco in the late 1970s, would fit this bill nicely. And if you pick up some fabulous makeup and styling tips

---

72. Hill and Thornley, *Principia Discordia*, 00061.

along the way, that'll just boost your Clown Witch mystique even further.

Peter J. Carroll once wrote that laughter is the highest emotion, since it can encompass all other emotions and has no opposite. And Phil Hine confirms that laughter is an effective form of ritual banishing, and that it can also be used "to deflate the pompous, self-important occult windbags that one runs into from time to time."[73] Plus, as Mal-2 once said, "Sometimes I take humor seriously. Sometimes I take seriousness humorously." Acknowledging the symbiosis of magic and humor, and in turn, acknowledging that you yourself are a magical, humorous being, will be a great leap forward as your own spirituality evolves.

---

73. Hine, *Oven-Ready Chaos*, 19.

Discordian Dance Break

Glamourbombs

Clown Witches are more than capable of binding or cursing, but they spiritually come into their own when their magic takes the form of what author and activist Hakim Bey branded poetic terrorism or what is known in some sparkling corners of the internet as glamourbombing. Originating as a concept in the Otherkin community, a glamourbomb is, according to Urban Dictionary, "Any public act or work that aims to inspire genuine curiosity and childlike befuddlement, a change of thought process, belief in magic, belief in the fae, and/or a sense of wonder in the recipient."[74] Glamourbombing often involves mundane, everyday items used or placed in an unusual manner. For example, leaving spare change on a sidewalk, but arranging the coins into a letter, number, or symbol. Or writing out vague but helpful advice on a notecard, signing it with the name of a god or an angel, and slipping it in between the pages of a random library book. Or giving out handmade holiday cards to strangers at any time other than the holiday season in question.

I once traced my hand on a wooden fence next to the parking lot of a late-night restaurant, drew a sigil in the palm, and scrawled Place Hand Here to Change Your Life above it. I also added Results May Vary in parentheses underneath it. The restaurant allowed customers to doodle on the fence (please keep in mind that vandalism is illegal). I don't know if anyone actually tried placing their hand there, but it remained on the fence well over a year before the restaurant repainted.

74. Spiritedust, "Glamourbomb."

exclusive radical feminist started hiccupping uncontrollably whenever she tried to say anything hateful? You know how, in *Practical Magic*, Gillian fixes it so that Sally ends up at the top of the phone tree? How might that translate into a chucklesome, real-world application?

What if every conspiracy theorist in your district got the date of Election Day wrong and showed up at the polling station a week after the fact?

Could Witchcraft bring about any of those situations? I can really only shrug in response, but I can also reiterate that you won't know until you try. And even if the magic doesn't work the way you expect it to, you'll still get some education in the process—and learning more about yourself and what you can do will always contribute toward your spiritual growth.

Chaos Spirituality 163

Of course, the Clown Witch could also choose to direct their glamourbombs into practical jokes with satirical edges that doubled as political statements—which, in Discordian spaces, would be known as a jake. For instance, what would happen if a far-right congressional representative's phone settings somehow glitched, and he could only tweet in Esperanto? What if a well-known trans-

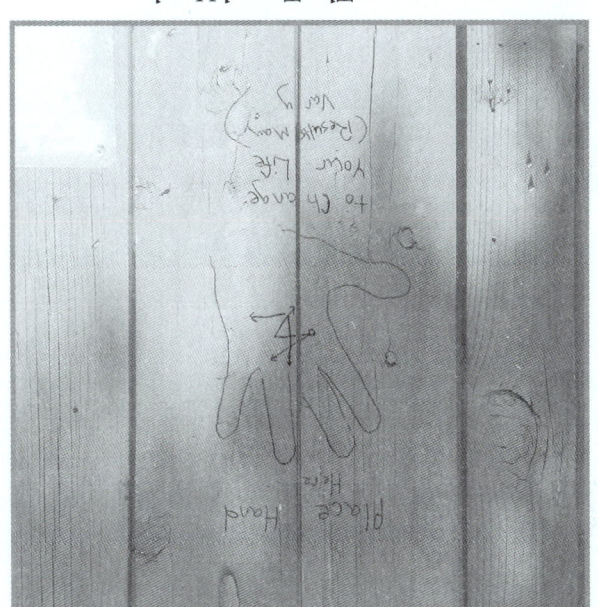

The Traced Hand

Shadow Work
[Insert Ominous Thunderclap Here]

As important as laughter is, though, both in Witchcraft and the mundane world, spirituality is not all fun and games. Becoming who we're supposed to be takes effort, and it is not a painless process. Which means it's time to discuss shadow work.

As hard as I try, I can't get away from shadow work. And by that, I mean no matter where I look, people *will not* stop talking about it. It has certainly become a popular term to bandy about, but it doesn't really seem to have much meaning behind it—or at least, it's being shoehorned into conversations without anyone really knowing what they mean when they say it. Are we talking about initiatory ordeals? Shamanic crises? Psychoanalysis? Cognitive-behavioral therapy? The Hero's Journey? All of these include concepts that *could* be described as shadow work, but there's not an overarching shadow work pennant under which we can cram them.

Let's dig a little into the origin of the term and find a definition we can actually use.

The Swiss psychiatrist Carl Jung defined the shadow as the unconscious part of the human psyche, similar to Sigmund Freud's concept of the Id. It's our animal nature, and it gives us the potential for both Creation and Destruction. As humans, we tend to reject or ignore the parts of ourselves we don't like, and those parts can become aspects of our shadows. Or, if we're wrestling with, say, low self-esteem, our shadows could be composed of positive things that don't gel with our negative self-image.

The goal of Jungian psychology, then, is to learn to acknowledge and accept the shadow, thus integrating the unconscious and the conscious selves into a Whole Person™. Which is nowhere near as easy as it sounds (and it honestly doesn't even sound that easy).

I am not quite sure how shadow work made the jump into modern Witchcraft, but it's currently as prevalent a topic as moon water and cord cutting. And while I do think actively working to integrate one's shadow can make one a healthier person and in turn a more competent and effective Witch, it's important to realize that a) it's a long-term process, not a one-time ritual, and b) it can be painful and scary and damaging.

And I really want to reiterate here that shadow work is, in the grand occult scheme of things, a very new concept. Medieval Witches were not all up in each other's business like, "It sounds liketh ye're goyng through somethyng, Rowena. Ye should really doon some shadowe werk about it."

If you want to pursue shadow work as part of your personal practice, that's awesome. In fact, Kelly-Ann Maddox offers some solid resources on shadow work in *Rebel Witch: Carve the Craft That's Yours Alone*, which I highly recommend. I personally got a lot out of *The Velvet Rage: Overcoming the Pain of Growing Up Gay in a Straight Man's World* by Alan Downs. It's not a self-help book per se, but it did help me identify some of the sources of my own internalized trauma and shame, which I was able to address through therapy and recovery.

Whatever you do, just keep in mind that as a psychological theory, shadow work is not Traditional Craft or anything. It's a tool that's compatible with Witchcraft, but it is emphatically not a requirement.

Searching and Fearless

Probably the best contemporary non-Witchcraft example of something that could be considered shadow work is 12-Step recovery, specifically Steps Four and Five:

Four—Made a searching and fearless moral inventory of ourselves.

Five—Admitted to [the] God[s], to ourselves, and to another human being the exact nature of our wrongs.[75]

In practice, a "searching and fearless moral inventory" means writing out a list of the people we resent, the reasons we resent them, the things those resentments affect (self-esteem, financial security, etc.), and "our part"—meaning what we've done to contribute to a given resentment, or why we're unable to let it go.

I am not exaggerating when I say this was one of the hardest things I've ever done.

Coming up with the list of people was actually easy, since I'd been internally categorizing them for years. The difficulty was looking at my part in those resentments. The more I wrote, the more I had to face that I was extremely entitled and thought the world owed me a lot of damn favors. And I ended up feeling like a really, really bad person.

But that's why those of us in recovery work with sponsors—recovering alcoholics who have already been through the Steps, and who can keep us moving forward and help us learn how to forgive ourselves and start healing. My own sponsor had me write out a fear inventory along with my resentments, which ultimately forced me to look at my untreated anxiety issues and do something about them. I probably wouldn't have sought treatment when I did if I hadn't had someone there to help me identify the problem and coax me into getting it managed.

The point here is that if you're going to engage in any kind of shadowy self-exploration, you need to do so with someone else

---

[75]. W., *Alcoholics Anonymous*, 59.

acting as a guide and/or spotter: a sponsor, a licensed therapist, or even a covenmate you trust implicitly. Trying to assimilate your unconscious without any kind of supervision or support—at least when you're first getting into it—will be ineffective at best and psychologically scarring at worst.

Once you've accomplished some integration with someone else tethering you, you can start doing work independently, like how those of us in recovery utilize Step Ten to "take personal inventory and when we were wrong promptly admitted it."[76]

If you're going to throw yourself into shadow work, my one nonnegotiable rule is this: Be kind to yourself. I mean it. Even with outside support, it's easy to slip into dark places when we're looking at the ugly parts of ourselves, so it is almost medically necessary that we treat ourselves as gently as possible while we're in the middle of it.

And you know what? If you never find a decent starting point, or if you just feel like shadow work isn't something you're interested in exploring, that's totally okay too. Above and beyond anything else, whether we're banging around the unconscious or not, we always need to be honest with ourselves. If your objective assessment is "no shadow work for me," then you're facing the situation and speaking your truth. And I cannot help but be proud of you for that.

Crafting with Chaos
A Step in the Right Direction

Another aspect of Step 4 is the fear inventory, which is exactly what it sounds like: writing out a comprehensive list of everything that scares you, along with the things

---

76. W., *Alcoholics Anonymous*, 59.

that those fears affect. Elevators were on my fear inventory. I've been cleithrophobic—afraid of being trapped or restrained—for as long as I can remember, and elevators exacerbate that phobia, which affected my self-esteem, pride, sense of security, and personal relationships. Cockroaches also made the list, as did fear of abandonment.

It was rough going, but I learned a couple of important things from the process—namely, that all fears are valid, and that I was not to blame for having those fears in the first place. Which was a big step toward letting them go.

Now, and only if you're feeling up to it, you're going to let go of a fear.

You will need

A makeup pencil (eyebrow or lip)

Baby wipes (preferably with aloe or other skin-soothing ingredients)

Directions

Think of a small fear: something you perceive as irrational. Maybe you're afraid that your favorite television show won't get renewed, or that someone in your workplace secretly doesn't appreciate your sense of style. Again, make sure it's something small—we're not trying to cure a panic disorder or anything with this exercise.

Once you have the fear in mind, come up with a sigil to represent it using one of the methods in chapter 7 or an outside method that works well for you. Using the makeup pencil, draw the sigil on your arm.

Blow on the sigil gently, and then, using one of the baby wipes, slowly remove the sigil, wiping away from yourself as you do so. Once the sigil is gone, wad up the wipe and throw it in the trash, then call your best friend and tell them about the fear, and the leap you took toward letting it go.

And after the spell is cast, relax, unwind, and reward yourself with a sweet treat.

Chapter 11
Chaos Divination

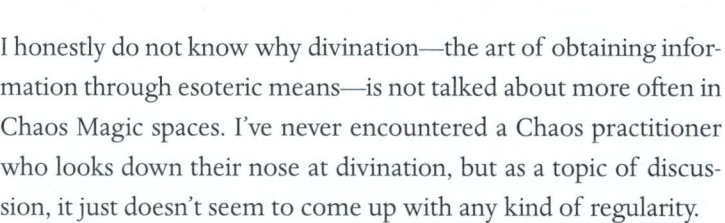

I honestly do not know why divination—the art of obtaining information through esoteric means—is not talked about more often in Chaos Magic spaces. I've never encountered a Chaos practitioner who looks down their nose at divination, but as a topic of discussion, it just doesn't seem to come up with any kind of regularity.

And that's a shame, because out of all the occult disciplines, divination is the one that really lends itself to Chaos Magic in general and Chaos Witchcraft in particular. After all, one of our key principles is Diversity in Approach, and divination provides a wild variety of methods with which to experiment.

That variety can be a bit overwhelming, so please remember that you don't have to become an expert in all of them—learning what you can about one or two systems will prove far more useful than trying to master thirty-two of them at once. But having a method of divination that grants consistently clear answers will be invaluable to you as a Witch, whether you want insight into what the results of a particular spell will be, receive a message from the gods and spirits you venerate, or just get an unbiased second opinion on a judgment call.

My own preferred method of divination is lithomancy—which means I read with semiprecious stones—and I've included a lithomantic tutorial later in this chapter. Regardless of the divinatory system that calls to you, there are techniques you can use to improve your skills. And if all else fails, you can peer into the future by simply listening to music, which we will get into in this chapter as well.

Divining Right In

Other Chaos principles that can be applied to divination are Immersion and Discipline—the metaphysical equivalent of starting a juice cleanse and sticking with it until you see results. And the best way to immerse yourself in divination and establish a disciplined practice is to construct a set of beliefs around a given divinatory system and nurture a unique, spiritual relationship with each card, rune, knucklebone, or whatever else is a standard tool of that system.

Once you've settled on a method of divination that you'd like to work with, choose a card/rune/etc. and place it in a prominent location in your home where you will see it every day. If you have an altar, you can put it there. For the next five days, learn everything you can about its symbolism. Make a concerted effort to see if you can identify the archetypes expressed by that symbol in the world around you. Also (and this is the hinge), set aside any other religious beliefs you may have, and treat that symbol like a deity in its own right. Pray to it, give it offerings, do whatever you would to venerate the gods of your personal pantheon.

After five days have passed, thank the symbol for what it taught you, then pull the next card or rune and start over, making that new symbol the center of your belief system.

Lenormadness Takes Control

To get a better picture of how to approach divination from an immersive and disciplined perspective, let's look at Lenormand playing cards, which derive from a late eighteenth-century parlor game called *The Game of Hope*.[77] Lenormand is not as well known as tarot, but it is a smaller deck with standardized images, so as an example, it will be easy to digest.

There are thirty-six cards in a traditional Lenormand deck, each associated with a regular playing card. The Lenormand cards are, in order:

1. The Rider (9H)
2. The Clover (6D)
3. The Ship (10S)
4. The Home (KH)
5. The Tree (7H)
6. The Clouds (KC)
7. The Snake (QC)
8. The Coffin (9D)
9. The Bouquet (QS)
10. The Scythe (JD)
11. The Birch Rod (JC)
12. The Birds (7D)
13. The Child (JS)
14. The Fox (9C)
15. The Bear (10C)
16. The Star (6H)

---

77. Matthews, *The Complete Lenormand Oracle Handbook*, 3–4.

17. The Stork (QH)
18. The Dog (10H)
19. The Tower (6S)
20. The Garden (8S)
21. The Mountain (8C)
22. The Crossroad (QD)
23. The Mice (7C)
24. The Heart (JH)
25. The Ring (AC)
26. The Book (10D)
27. The Letter (7S)
28. The Gentleman (AH)
29. The Lady (AS)
30. The Lily (KS)
31. The Sun (AD)
32. The Moon (8H)
33. The Key (8D)
34. The Fish (KD)
35. The Anchor (9D)
36. The Cross (6C)

To start developing your relationship with the Lenormand system, you'll begin with the Rider (indicative of news, visitors, luggage, and a potential love interest if the querent is attracted to men). For five days, you'll absorb as much knowledge as possible about the Rider, and any prayers or petitions you might have will be addressed to him, those petitions being specific to the concepts he represents. For instance, if you're in the market for a new boyfriend, the Rider would be the right spirit to invoke.

In a Lenormand spread, cards are often read in pairs, so you'll also want to use this time to familiarize yourself with the different ways the Rider interacts with other symbols. (A journal is going to be indispensable for this experiment.) Additionally, you'll keep an eye out for any appearances of the Rider in your day-to-day life, paying special attention to arrivals, be they packages or people. And when those five days are up, you'll give thanks to the Rider for spending the week with you, leaving a small token of gratitude for him. (Nine candy hearts would be appropriate.) The following morning, you'll pull out the Clover card and repeat the entire process.

In taking on this pilgrimage, you will find that some of the spirits will be easy to interact with, while others will present challenges. And you may feel like you're putting extraneous restrictions on yourself, or uselessly capping your own abilities, which, in a way, you are. But you're also building from the ground up within an alien paradigm and figuring out how to orient yourself—the longer you work with your oracle and its associated spirits, the more room you'll have to grow and experiment. After sojourning through the entire system, you'll be able to come back to your original practice much more adept at divination.

I'll tell you, though: It will get uncomfortable. It's one thing to move back and forth between, say, non-initiatory Wicca and nondenominational Paganism—they're similar enough in praxis that you won't get carsick jumping from one to the other. But in this new belief system, there may not be any familiar touchstones. Want to check in with Eris? Oops, sorry. Try again when the Snake card comes up. Longing for a ritual tool? You've got a Scythe and a Birch Rod. Go crazy with that.

Discipline means working through the cards in order, giving each the same amount of your attention, and not skipping ahead to the cards you think will be more useful or interesting. But it's an exciting process, even if it's also a little scary. It's like going on safari, or wandering into an old building full of ghosts and weird antiques. Belief is a tool, after all, and once you make it all the way through your deck or your stones or what have you, you will have a nifty, finely tuned utensil to incorporate into your Chaos Witchcraft. Plus, you may find that you have a lot more appreciation for the tools already in your possession. And having survived the experience, you will be good and seasoned and ready to throw yourself into another one.

Chaos Rocks

A big part of approaching magic from the perspective of a Chaos Witch is being aware of the boundaries and limitations of any given situation, and then figuring out ways to make stuff happen within them, or to circumvent them all together. It's not always so much about shifting the paradigm as it is rewiring the paradigm from the inside.

And a really solid opportunity to see Chaos Magical Theory in action comes from lithomancy, my all-time favorite method of divination. I touched on lithomancy in the book *Virgo Witch*, but I want to go more in depth with it here, to emphasize that Chaos Magic is more than just sigils and servitors—it's diving into any field that interests you, metaphysical or otherwise, learning whatever you can, then putting your new knowledge to work to see what kind of results you get, and to see if those results can be repeated.

There are historical accounts of lithomantic divination, although the practice looked very different from how it's usually depicted today—it was basically just, *Find a good rock and listen for the screams.* The ninth-century Roman physician Eusebius, for example, had a chunk of meteorite he called a baetelum that would allegedly emit shrill sounds, which he could interpret and use to help diagnose patients, and the Greek seer Helenus owned a lodestone, which had been given to him by Apollo, and which would speak in the voice of a child.[78] According to myth (and to slide in a reference to Discordianism wherever I can), the lodestone was able to warn Helenus of the impending fall of Troy.

Modern, non-audial lithomancy was first promoted by Doreen Valiente in her 1978 book *Witchcraft for Tomorrow*, and I have found that it's a much more effective method of divination than just sitting around and waiting for the stones to clap back. As Valiente describes, "It requires thirteen stones, the typical witches' number, namely seven stones for the seven planets, plus a life stone, a luck stone, a love stone, a home stone, a news stone, and a magic stone."[79]

The stones are divided into two categories: planetary and personal. The planetary meanings are:

Sun—Energy, cheerfulness, vitality, and authority figures.

Moon—Emotions, change, intuition, and maternal figures.

Mercury—Communication, intelligence, strategy, gambling, and a nonbinary person.

Venus—Unions, harmony, fidelity, happiness, and a woman.

Mars—Strife, courage, defense, conflict, and a man.

Jupiter—Money, authority, justice, and prosperity.

Saturn—Restriction, delay, purification, and longevity.

And the personal meanings are:

---

78. Howard, *Pagan Portals*, 4.
79. Valiente, *Witchcraft for Tomorrow*, 93.

Life—Milestone events, nature, physical and mental health, and things one can't control.

Luck—Chance occurrences, passion, willpower, and outside assistance.

Love—Intimacy, compassion, healing, and reconciliation.

Home—Security, personal property, family, and friends.

News—Information, wishes, hopes and dreams, and inspiration.

Magic—The ruling factor, the unexpected, timing, and the Divine.

To perform a reading, make a circle on a table or the floor with a length of cord; the circle should have a diameter of roughly a foot and a half, just to give the stones room to spread out. Trace along the inside of the circle with your finger to smooth out any bumps or kinks in the cord, then (gently) toss or drop the stones into the center of the circle. The Magic stone is the Indicator, and yes-no questions are answered by the Jupiter and Saturn stones—if the Indicator is closer to Jupiter, the answer is yes; if it's closer to Saturn, the answer is no; and if it lands equidistant between Jupiter and Saturn, the answer is maybe.

As for the rest of the stones, Valiente encouraged the reader to use their intuition, which is either brutally unhelpful or refreshingly liberating, depending on your point of view. Personally, I see it as liberating—and over the years, other lithomancers have developed some useful techniques to explain what the stones have to say in various positions.

Start off by locating the Indicator and determine if it's closer to Jupiter or Saturn. This will tell you if the overall reading is favorable or unfavorable. After that, look at the other nearby stones, and see if their meanings clarify the favorability/unfavorability. Finally, look for clusters of stones, and the shapes made by those clusters.

Straight horizontal or vertical lines suggest linear progressions of events. Diagonal lines can represent progressions of events that are connected, even if they appear unrelated at first glance. Curves indicate resistance (upward), or lack thereof (downward). Triangles mean that everything is in place for the querent (that is, the person you're reading for) to move forward. The stones comprising the triangle will tell you what those things are. Squares mean that certain factors need to come together as a foundation for the querent to move forward, but those factors are not in place yet. The stones comprising the square will tell you what those factors are.

It will definitely take some practice to interpret your lithomantic spreads, but once you get a feel for it, it can be a surprisingly accurate method of divination. When you're starting out, stick to yes-no readings until you have a good feel for things, then branch out and start focusing your attention on the various patterns created by the positions of the other stones, which will yield answers like, "Yes, and here's why," and, "No, because of these factors."

ACWAP

Now that you've got the fundamentals down, let's do some rearranging to make lithomancy ACWAP (As Chaos Witchcraft As Possible).

Since the classical planets correspond to the colors of the sephiroth in Hermetic Qabalah, and those colors are represented by the arrows of the Chaos Star, I'm going to move the Magic stone to the Planetary column so that all eight arrows are represented. Additionally, the Personal stones are sometimes equated with the classical Elements, which means they also have Discordian Elemental counterparts.

If you incorporate these Chaos and Discordian concepts into your lithomancy, and you change the planetary and personal headers to *magical* and *elemental*, here's what you end up with:

Sun—Ego

Moon—Sex

Mercury—Thinking

Venus—Partnership

Mars—War

Jupiter—Wealth

Saturn—Death

Magic—Magic

Life—Boom

Luck—Orange

Love—Sweet

Home—Prickle

News—Pungent

The core meanings of the stones remain the same, but now you have very specific keywords for your readings. Additionally, the personal/elemental stones can represent things that can be heard, seen, tasted, touched, and smelled.

Now, regarding the materials of the stones themselves, Valiente has this to say: "My own set of stones consists of a mixture of stones which I have found and those which I have bought…[O]ne's set of divining stones should be individual to oneself, satisfying one's own idea of what is right in this way and appealing to one's own inner mind."[80]

What this tells us is that *stone* doesn't have to be taken literally—any small objects of roughly the same size and shape will work for lithomantic divination. I started out with antique marbles that originally belonged to my father and grandfather, and I eventually graduated to gaming dice: ten-sided dice for Death, Wealth, Partnership, Ego, Sex, Thinking, and War; an eight-sided die for Pungent; a twelve-sided die for Sweet; a six-sided die for Prickle; a four-sided die for Orange; and twenty-sided dice for Boom and Magic.

And while I do use actual stones as my primary lithomantic tools, I still enjoy using gaming dice, since their varied shapes and edges mean that they can clearly point to each other, adding a directional flow to the information presented in readings. Plus I'll only be out a few cents if I ever need to replace one of them. I also have an irrational but deep-seated aversion to tabletop role-playing games, so working something traditionally associated with TTRPGs into my Witchcraft forces me out of my self-imposed comfort zone.

As a postscript, the magic words Valiente provides—to be chanted three times before casting the stones—are *ADA ADA IO ADA DIA*.[81] Valiente believed that they derived from Welsh, and there's a chance they might actually be corrupted Welsh Romani. But I once altered them to *ADA ADA IO ADA ERIS*, and I'll be darned if my next reading wasn't clear as a bell. Give it a try yourself and see what you think.

---

80. Valiente, *Witchcraft for Tomorrow*, 94.
81. Valiente, *Witchcraft for Tomorrow*, 96.

Translated into their Chaos keywords and read together, the stones were proclaiming, "NO. EGO WAR."

I was already pretty sold on lithomancy before this experience, but the fact that the stones wanted in on the joke endeared them to me forever.

Discordian Dance Break
Conversational Chaos

A friend and I once ended up in a very facetious online feud, which has pretty much refused to die, mainly because we both think it's hysterical. The *faux* animosity started organically; I was on a social media app mouthing off about whatever aspect of modern occultism was bugging me at the moment, and, just for grins, he commented on that post with melodramatic outrage, threatening to put a curse on me for my insolence.

In response, I told him that I'd just received an unexpected cash windfall, so if he'd like to curse me again, I could also use a new set of tires, please and thank you. He retorted with an invocation to the Old Ones, I countered with the Turkey Curse, and our mutual acquaintances cheered in delight and egged us both on. (Although there are a handful of people out there who never figured out that the feud was not real and, to this day, fully believe we're mortal enemies. The next time my friend and I meet in person, one of us is going to have to punch the other in the face just to keep up appearances.)

A few months later, I started experimenting with using the forms of magic as lithomantic keywords, and to stress-test my theories, I hopped back online and asked if anyone had some sample questions I could try to answer.

The friend in question was one of the first to leave a comment: "Will our feud ever come to an end?" he queried.

"Well, I certainly hope not," I thought, but I went ahead and threw the stones anyway. The indicator landed right next to Saturn, with the Sun and Mars coupled directly beneath it.

Shufflemancy

When I was in college, I used music to regulate my mood. I had a stack of frenetically upbeat dance hits that I listened to when I wanted to cheer myself up, as well as a mixtape of tear-jerking ballads that I would play whenever I was feeling a little *too* happy and needed to simmer down a bit. There were a couple of albums I only listened to when it was time to study, plus my friends could tell if I was having a good or bad day based on which act of the *Rent* original cast recording was blasting from my dorm.

If I'd have put all these songs together in one collection, I would have had an oracle.

Shufflemancy is an emerging form of divination that involves extracting answers from music. It's a new enough practice that there are no set rules, which makes it ideal as a tool for the Chaos Witch: You get to decide entirely how to make it work best for you. The only thing you will need is an option to play a random song on demand, without knowing which song it will be until you hear it.

A good way to get going with shufflemancy is to put together a playlist, including at least twenty songs. You'll want a variety of genres and artists on your playlist, so that the answers you receive aren't too generalized. You'll also want to make sure there's an even mix of favorable and unfavorable tracks—there should be some songs that you love and represent yes to you, but others that give a clear no, and at least one or two that you can't stand.

Once your playlist is complete, think of a question, then put the list on shuffle and note the title of the first song that starts playing. Listen to the song all the way through, paying close attention to the lyrics, and accept the information that is presented to you.

You can add to or subtract from your playlist whenever you'd like. Just be sure to keep a solid balance of yes and no, favorable and unfavorable, happy and sad. And again, there are no rules to shufflemancy, but I would recommend keeping this particular playlist set aside for divinatory purposes only. You don't want to get so used to hearing the songs on it that you miss anything important they're trying to tell you.

Now, if you don't have the ability or resources to put playlists together, you can still practice shufflemancy out in the wild. Sometimes, if I have a certain question in mind, I'll wait until I have to drive somewhere, then turn on my car radio and interpret whatever song happens to be playing. I've also received shufflemantic messages via the music playing in a department store, a store coincidentally being the location of the greatest example of shufflemancy I've ever witnessed.

I was shopping for clothes one day, digging around and looking for deals, when another customer a row over from me pulled a fetching but tight-looking shirt off the rack.

He turned to a nearby mirror and held the shirt up to his chest, and right then, the song "Lose Control" by Teddy Swims began playing on the overhead.

The customer stopped and cocked his head, listening intently to the opening lyrics. "That's a bad omen," he said, to himself but out loud. And he put the shirt back on the rack and walked away.

There are omens and portents all around us. With some practice and a little discernment, you will be able to determine which ones are meant for you, and you'll have all the information you need to act accordingly.

Crafting with Chaos
Spreading the Love

Once you have a solid relationship with the oracle of your choice, you can start experimenting with different layouts and configurations, eventually devising your own to get tailored answers to any questions you have in mind. Following is a spread I came up with, based on the Discordian seasons, to use with my Lenormand cards. See if it works for you, but also feel free to edit it, move the positions around, or make it the basis of a template no one has ever seen before.

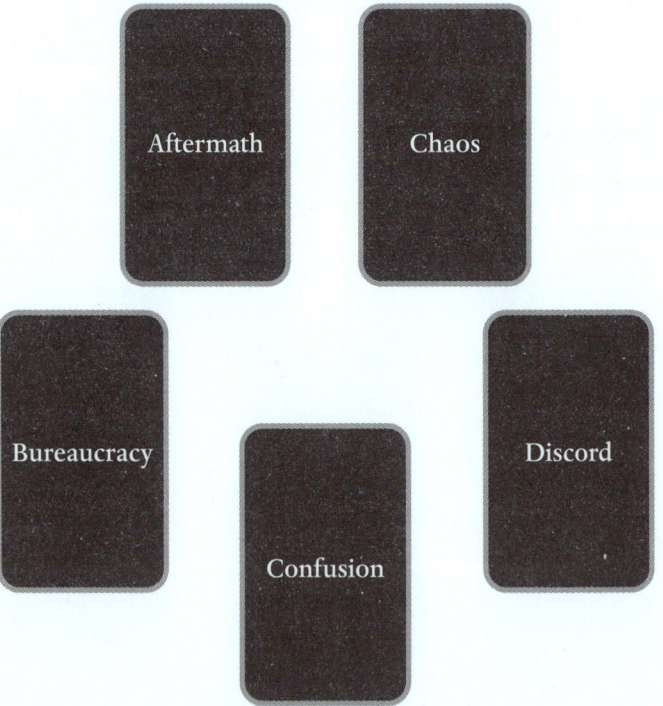

The Discordian Seasons Layout

Here are the steps to the spread as I use it:

1. Shuffle your deck at least five times.
2. Pull a card and lay it in front of you. This is the Chaos card, which represents the origin or backstory of the situation at hand.
3. Pull a second card and place it just below and to the right of the Chaos card. This is the Discord card, which tells you what information about the situation is readily available. It also will warn of any potential conflicts.
4. Pull a third card and place it to the left of the Discord card. This is the Confusion card, which indicates what's not being seen regarding the situation, or what is currently hidden.
5. Pull a fourth card and place it to the left of the Confusion card. This is the Bureaucracy card, which indicates any obstacles that may be encountered, or any issues that will need to be dealt with before the querent can move forward.
6. Pull a fifth card and place it above and just to the right of the Bureaucracy card. This is the Aftermath card, which reveals the resolution or final outcome.

This is a solid, workable method of Discordian divination, if I do say so myself. But if you want to get even more Discordian with it, I have a bonus procedure for you.

1. Clear your mind of any questions.
2. Yell, "Hey, Eris," with as much force as you can muster.

3. Throw your oracle deck (or an *Uno* deck, or a *Cards Against Humanity* deck) into the air.
4. Pick five random cards that have fallen facedown.
5. Flip them over and read them in any order. Therein will lie the answer.

Chapter 12
Holydays and Astrology

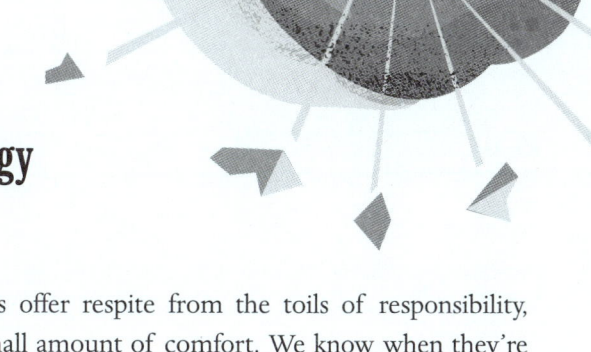

Religious festivals offer respite from the toils of responsibility, along with no small amount of comfort. We know when they're coming, which can be a touchtone in an otherwise unpredictable world, and preparing for them often involves as much merriment as the celebrations themselves.

These special days can be solemn occasions as well, as those who observe look back on the year behind them or memorialize the people or things that are no longer with them. And sometimes, they are just excuses to cut loose and carouse, to act silly for no other reason than it is, at that moment, time to act silly.

The best festivals reflect all of that, and Discordianism provides a plethora. Let's walk our way through them and see what we can learn—not only about the Discordian worldview, but about ourselves.

A Decagon of Derangement

Each Discordian season features a *Holyday* on its fifth and fiftieth day—the former being the feast of the Discordian Apostle who governs the season, and the latter acknowledging the season itself before the next season begins.

The Holydays, with their Discordian and corresponding Gregorian dates, are as follows:

Mungday—Chaos 5 (January 5)

Chaoflux—Chaos 50 (February 19)

Mojoday—Discord 5 (March 19)

Discoflux—Discord 50 (May 3)

Syaday—Confusion 5 (May 31)

Confuflux—Confusion 50 (July 15)

Zaraday—Bureaucracy 5 (August 12)

Bureflux—Bureaucracy 50 (September 26)

Maladay—Aftermath 5 (October 24)

Afflux—Aftermath 50 (December 8)

Although the Holydays are listed in the *Principia Discordia*, the book does not provide any information on how to celebrate them, which is a challenge. But since you're practicing Chaos Witchcraft, and you've got the skills to construct your own belief systems, you can do with the Holydays whatever you'd like—you'll just want to stick to the spirit of each Apostle and season as you move through the calendar.

Here are my humble suggestions.

Mungday—The Fifth Day of Chaos (January 5)

Since it's the first Holyday of the year, Mungday is the right time to set goals for the upcoming months. Use your favorite divination methods to glimpse what the year holds for you, and take some time to meditate on the Sacred Chao, depicted on page 53, in which a pentagon represents rigid Order and a golden apple represents flexible Disorder, and think about them in terms of problems and solutions. What pentagons are currently in your way? What apples do you have at your disposal?

Hung Mung is traditionally depicted laughing, slapping his knee (or buttocks) and declaring "I don't know!" in response to anything asked of him, so Mungday customs may include laughing maniacally at inappropriate moments and ritualistically stage-slapping oneself in Hung Mung's honor. In the world of computing, *mung* is jargon for making repeated changes to a file, resulting in unintentional but irreversible Destruction. If you're handy with coding, or if you have a talent for unwittingly downloading malware, you can celebrate Mungday by "accidentally" crashing computers, then calling your company's IT department and yelling "I don't know!" every time they ask you what happened.

Fun fact: The dwarf planet Eris was discovered on Mungday 2005, marking the official recognition of the physical presence of Our Lady of Discord in the universe.

Gospel Reading for Mungday

"[I]n times of medieval magic, the pentagon was the generic symbol for werewolves, but this reference is not particularly intended and it should be noted that the Erisian Movement does not discriminate against werewolves—our membership roster is open to persons of all races, national origins and hobbies."—*Principia Discordia*, page 00051

Chaoflux—The 50th Day of Chaos (February 19)

Chaoflux is a day to make decisions, and to start taking action toward the goals you set on Mungday: Blow cinnamon through your front door, as described in the introduction of this book. Or, if you're feeling noncommittal, Chaoflux offers the chance to change your mind at the last minute and come up with different goals entirely.

The Season of Chaos is coming to a close, which means Chaos itself will soon congeal into organized form. Subtle signs of Discord are appearing, like the first blades of grass poking out of a snowbank... if, you know, the grass was kind of snippy and dyspeptic. Chaoflux is a lot like Imbolc—also known as Candlemas, the Gaelic fire festival marking the end of winter and the beginning of spring—just without any fire hazards or inadvertent Catholicism.

Gospel Reading for Chaoflux

"The Earthquakes and the heavens rattle; the beasts of nature flock together and the nations of men flock apart; volcanoes usher up heat while elsewhere water becomes ice and melts; and then on other days it just rains. Indeed do many things come to pass."—*Principia Discordia*, page 00014

Mojoday—The Fifth Day of Discord (March 19)

Mojoday presents an opportunity to stretch your boundaries and step out of your comfort zone. Dr. Van Van Mojo is sometimes said to dress in tweed suits and death masks, and to surround himself with a cloud of blue smoke, so feel free to do the same—or at the very least, give yourself a temporary, radical makeover, or go out in public wearing a cunning disguise. In keeping with the season, your Mojoday celebration should also include a passionate, inappropriately timed argument over who should or should not be venerated.

Meet up with a like-minded friend and lightly anoint yourselves with apple juice, then travel to a semipublic, Aneristic destination, like a bank lobby, a waiting room, a commuter train station, the DMV, or Bingo Night. Flip a coin to determine which one of you is Team Van Van Mojo, and who is Team Patamunzo Lingananda. Remember that some Discordians venerate Patamunzo Lingananda instead of Dr. Mojo, as discussed in chapter 4. Immediately switch teams.

Start squabbling, with arguments including obscure quotations from as many obscure Discordian works as possible (*The Callipygian Grimoire*, for example, or *The Final Magnum Opiate of Alynaar the Shattered*). Both parties should try their best to baffle the innocent bystanders around them before demanding that they all pick sides.

Gospel Reading for Mojoday

"Lord Omar claims that Dr. Mojo heaps hatred upon Patamunzo, who sends only Love Vibrations in return. But we of the POEE sect know that Patamunzo is the Real Imposter, and that those vibrations of his are actually an attempt to subvert Dr. Mojo's rightful apostilic authority by shaking him out of his wits."—*Principia Discordia*, page 00039

Discoflux—The 50th Day of Discord (May 3)

If you put magical effort toward your annual goals, portents may begin to make themselves known around Discoflux, so keep an eye out for signs that your magic is working. And if those signs are not yet visible, or if they're indecipherable, do not lose heart. Lust of result may start to feel like a viable option as the Season of Confusion begins creeping in—best to practice your nonattachment, let your magic do its work, and enjoy the jubilee.

As for how the day should be commemorated, consensus suggests that the *disco* in *Discoflux* should be taken literally, and I cannot support this enough. Break out your bell-bottoms, feather your hair, do the Hustle, watch *Saturday Night Fever*, use a mirror ball to tell fortunes. Live fully in the 1970s, if only for twenty-four hours.

I was once lucky enough to see Thelma Houston in concert, and right before she sang her 1976 dance hit "Don't Leave Me This Way," she told the audience that when she was nominated for a Grammy, she didn't think she would win, so she didn't attend the award show. As such, she found out that she'd won Best Female R&B Vocal Performance while she was scrubbing her kitchen floor.

"The moral of this story," Houston said, "is that if you ever get nominated for a Grammy, *you go*." Which is pretty motivating advice for Discoflux as well.

Gospel Reading for Discoflux

"Mal began to laugh. Omar began to jump up and down. Mal was hooting and hollering to beat all hell. And amid squeals of mirth and with tears on their cheeks, each appointed the other to be high priest of his own madness, and together they declared themselves to be a society of Discordia, for what ever that may turn out to be."—*Principia Discordia*, page 00010

Syaday—The Fifth Day of Confusion (May 31)

Sri Syadasti is the patron of all things psychedelic, so the first step in celebrating Syaday is altering your consciousness in whatever manner you're comfortable with. Sobriety limits my options, so

I usually follow Step 11—"Sought through prayer and meditation to improve our conscious contact with God[s] as we understand God[s]"—and just trance out under my own volition.[82] And don't forget that there are excitatory ways to achieve gnosis as well—see how many jumping jacks you can do, in sets of fifty. Regardless of how you get there, once you're good and blurry, chant Syadasti's full name five hundred times.

In honor of the season, though, you do need to make things confusing. Be sure to lose count while you're chanting, or switch back and forth arbitrarily between English and Sanskrit. If you regularly utilize prayer beads while meditating, hold them in your nondominant hand, or put them around your ankle and move the beads with your nondominant toes. Forget what you're chanting; forget what you're doing. Get distracted. Realize halfway through your meditation that you don't know where your keys are. Call an old friend and suddenly remember to start chanting again. Forget to hang up.

As Eris once said, there is no tyranny in the State of Confusion, so be egalitarian and bring as many people as you can along on your trip. Whether he's fictitious or St. Gulik or somewhere in between, Sri Syadasti will hold the doors open for all of you.

Gospel Reading for Syaday

"Tell constricted mankind that there are no rules, unless they choose to invent rules. Keep close the words of Syadasti: *'Tis an ill wind that blows no minds*. And remember that there is no tyranny in the State of Confusion. For further information, consult your pineal gland."—*Principia Discordia*, page 00009

---

82. W., *Alcoholics Anonymous*, 59.

Confuflux—The 50th Day of Confusion (July 15)

Confuflux distinguishes itself from other Discordian Holydays by being the hardest to pronounce. And since it's the halfway point of the year, it's an appropriate time to take stock of your goals, and evaluate which ones you are actively accomplishing, and which ones may need some revision.

Malaclypse the Younger once affirmed, "We Discordians must stick apart," meaning that we should revel in our differences and find unity in diversity, and that we don't all have to do things the same way. This is something worth exploring on Confuflux: Interact with other Chaos Witches today and compare notes. Discuss the compositions of your practices, trade tips, and draw inspiration from one another.

When out and about on Confuflux, you can celebrate by sowing as much actual confusion as possible, whether through your dress or confounding but harmless behavior. Today is also a great day to get lost in your city of residence: Head off in a random direction, make random turns, and ignore the desperate pleadings of your GPS until you end up in a part of town to which you've never been before. Locate a gas station or convenience store, ask for directions back to your neighborhood, and buy an outlandish hat.

Gospel Reading for Confuflux

"Go ye hence and lift the Stash, that ye may come to own it and, owning it, share it and, sharing it, love in it and, loving in it, dwell in it and, dwelling in the Stash, become a Poet of the Word and a Sayer of Sayings—an Inspiration to all men and a Scribe to the Gods."—*Principia Discordia*, page 00048

Zaraday—The Fifth Day of Bureaucracy (August 12)

Zarathud once lost an argument to a cow, and to commemorate that great moment in Discordian history, cut your losses and accept defeats today.[83] If one of your goals is just not working out, let it go and focus on those that are still in progress.

As the harbinger of the Season of Bureaucracy, Zaraday is not quite as celebratory as the other Holydays—after all, Bureaucracy is established Confusion; the implementation of complex systems that continually break down and cause more problems. And that's...not particularly enjoyable. As such, the best way to observe Zaraday is to just tackle whatever tedious chores or responsibilities you've been putting off and get them over and done with.

Fold the laundry, clean out your refrigerator, read your HOA deed restrictions, go through your email and unsubscribe from all the spam, and update all your passwords. It won't be fun, and it probably won't even be that rewarding, but at least it will be finished. If anything, you can think of whatever burden you overcome as an offering to Zarathud. And I will appreciate that, even if he's too caught up in debating livestock to notice.

Gospel Reading for Zaraday

"The Pentabarf was discovered by the hermit Apostle Zarathud in the Fifth Year of The Caterpillar. He found them carved in gilded stone, while building a sun deck for his cave, but their import was lost for they were written in a mysterious cypher. However, after ten weeks and eleven hours of intensive scrutiny he discerned that the message could be read by standing on his head and viewing it upside down."—*Principia Discordia*, page 00004

---

83. Hill and Thornley, *Principia Discordia*, 00048.

Bureflux—The 50th Day of Bureaucracy (September 26)

The Curse of Greyface is most powerful during the Season of Bureaucracy, which is highlighted by paperwork and longer-than-average hold times. But Bureflux brings a fleeting sense of optimism—we've only got twenty-three days left until the next Discordian season, so all the red tape that Eris is currently using as aerial silk is almost behind us.

To put it succinctly, Bureflux is an Equinox and a retrograde rolled into one. And out of all the Holydays, Bureflux is the only one that exhausts me: I have a tough time coming up with anything interesting to say about it. Which might actually be the point, now that I think about it.

Just be nice to yourself today. Indulge in some self-care, avoid any shadow work, and don't check your DMs.

Gospel Reading for Bureflux

"As a public service to all mankind and civilization in general, and to us in particular, the Golden Apple Corps has concluded that planning such a Pilgrimage [to the bowling alley where Eris first revealed herself] is sufficient and that it is prudent to never get around to actually going."—*Principia Discordia*, page 00060

Maladay—The Fifth Day of Aftermath (October 24)

Discord leads to Confusion, which crystallizes into Bureaucracy, which in turn creates an unsustainable system—eventually, it collapses into Aftermath, which is where we find ourselves today. But that's a good thing, since Destruction always leads to Creation: Every time Aneris takes something away, Eris creates something new to replace it.

And since the Elder Malaclypse is such a fan of conspiracies, I think the perfect way to honor him on his special day is to create some new ones.

Another traditional (insofar as anything within Discordianism can be called traditional) method of celebrating Maladay is to play the game Flip the Table, the origins of which are allegedly attributed to the Elder Malaclypse himself. Any number of participants can play: All you need is two to twenty-three friends and a table, preferably covered with symbols of Bureaucracy (overdue bills, user manuals, Windows 10, etc.).

With appropriate music in the background, players grab hold of the table and, on cue, lift and toss, with the goal of causing the table to land in an interesting, unexpected way. Players may also wish to scry in the patterns of debris left over once the table and its contents hit the ground.

Flip the Table can really be played at any time during the Season of Aftermath, although protests and riots make the game more entertaining and meaningful. Try throwing the table through a police barricade for extra points, or attempt a variation in which whoever traps the most flat-earthers under a table wins.

Reinvent the rules however you'd like, or just reinvent yourself. It's Aftermath, and there are pieces everywhere, so pick them up and put them together however you see fit. I wholeheartedly believe that the Elder Malaclypse will be wildly entertained by whatever you create.

Gospel Reading for Maladay

"From that moment of illumination, a man begins to be free regardless of his surroundings. He becomes free to play order games and change them at will. He becomes free to play disorder games just for the hell of it. He becomes free to play neither or both. And as the master of his own games, he plays without fear, and therefore without frustration, and therefore with good will in his soul and love in his being."—*Principia Discordia*, page 00081

Afflux—The 50th Day of Aftermath (December 8)

Afflux is the closest thing Discordians have to a Winter Solstice. It marks the close of the calendar year, which makes it a good time to reflect on the relationship between Creation and Destruction, to examine the things that have come undone around us, and to figure out what we can do with the pieces. Look back over any goals you may have jettisoned on Zaraday, determine why they failed to launch, and figure out another angle toward achieving them.

Afflux is a day of putting things back together. Solving jigsaw puzzles would be a low-key way to celebrate the Holyday, as would baking, if you think about it in terms of taking a bunch of random, unrelated substances and welding them together into a tasty, unified whole.

I am a terror in the kitchen, so personally, I stick to borrowing from Yom Kippur—the Jewish day of atonement—by patching up any friendships that have fallen by the wayside. But if you can pull something out of the oven without setting off a fire alarm, then knock yourself out, with my blessing.

If you have the materials on hand, kintsugi—the Japanese art of repairing broken pottery with gold lacquer—would also be a meaningful way to commemorate Afflux. The philosophy behind kintsugi is that breakages are part of an object's story: By using gold to fix the cracks, the damaged item becomes more beautiful for what it's been through.

And if you don't have any broken crockery lying around, feel free to smash a coffee mug or something, then glue it back together however you want. Build something entirely new out of it—turn it into an abstract sculpture, or a self-defense weapon, or even a ritual tool. Acknowledge how the breaks in your own past have made you stronger in the long run, and how they have allowed you to reinvent yourself.

Beam that same intention into the ceramic shards in front of you. And use them to make something beautiful.

Gospel Reading for Afflux

"During and after the Fall of the Establishment of Bureaucracy was the Aftermath, an Age of Disorder in which calculation, computations, and reckonings were put away by the Children of Eris in Acceptance and Preparation for the Return to Oblivion to be followed by a Repetition of the Universal Absurdity. Moreover, of Itself the Coming of Aftermath waseth a Resurrection of the Freedom-flowing Chaos."—*Principia Discordia*, page 00045

Discordian Dance Break

Chelseanacht

On July 17, 2007, members of the loose-knit occult organization that eventually became known as the Domus Kaotica Marauder Underground performed an act of conjoint long-distance magic. The DKMU wanted to put the Chaos (specifically the Khaos, which they understood to be the source code of reality) back in Chaos Magic: On the night in question, four practitioners—one in Texas, one in California, one in Maryland, and one atop the Chelsea Hotel in New York City—worked together to create an "assault on reality."[84] Their objective was to shake things up, break open new magics, and jumpstart an epic, subconscious mass deconditioning.

Every July 17 since then, Chaotes collaborate with each other to honor the anniversary of the Chelsea Working. Chaos Witches tend to lean toward solitary practice, but Chelseanacht offers the opportunity to experiment with group work. In the weeks leading up to July 17, organize through social media, settle on a collective desire, synchronize your watches, and discover what kind of results a one-night-only coven can achieve.

---

84. Roger, "About the DKMU," 84–85.

Discordian Astrology
(or, Giving Birth to Dancing Stars)

There are several religious holidays that are inexorably linked to astronomical and astrological phenomena. In Wicca, for example, Yule is the celebration of the return of the sun, since days start getting longer after the Winter Solstice. And in Catholicism, the date of Easter changes every year, because it is always held on the first Sunday after the first Full Moon after the Spring Equinox, which the Church officially recognizes as March 21.[85]

With ten distinct Holydays of its own, it would be reasonable to assume that Discordianism has some kind of connection to astrology, and in fact, page 00063 of the *Principia* highlights the details of the official Discordian Astrological System. Here is that passage in its entirety:

1. On your next birthday, return to the place of your birth and, at precisely midnight, noting your birth time and date of observation, count all visible stars.
2. When you have done this, write to me and I'll tell you what to do next.

Like so many other facets of Discordianism, the Astrological System is a punch line: It emphasizes the elaborate and often perplexing nature of traditional astrology before poking some fun at it. At the same time, Discordian astrology could be a fascinating field of study—if anything, it could offer some insight into why Chaos Witches are, well, the way we are.

I have very thoughtfully invented it.

---

85. Carter, "Why Does Easter Change Dates?"

Just as it is based on five seasons, the Discordian calendar sports five-day weeks, with each day of the week named after one of the five Elements. These days are:

Sweetmorn

Boomtime

Pungenday

Prickle-Prickle

Setting Orange

The Discordian calendar is static, and the days of the week do not shift from year to year—for example, the fifteenth of May will always fall on Setting Orange, no matter what. This means that the first step in determining your Discordian astrological sign is to figure out the day of the week on which you were born. You can refer to the calendar in chapter 4. Once you know your day, you will have the first half of your sign: your ruling Element.

Once you've got your day, look back at the calendar and note the season in which you were born. This season is the second half of your sign, which will also tell you which Apostle of Eris is your patron. As a refresher, here are the Apostles and their seasons:

Hung Mung, Patron of Chaos

Dr. Van Van Mojo, Patron of Discord

Sri Syadasti, Patron of Confusion

Zarathud, Patron of Bureaucracy

The Elder Malaclypse, Patron of Aftermath

And this means that instead of the paltry twelve of the Zodiac, Discordianism is replete with twenty-five distinct astrological signs.

The Discordian Astrological Signs

Sweetmorn of Chaos
Sweetmorn of Discord
Sweetmorn of Confusion
Sweetmorn of Bureaucracy
Sweetmorn of Aftermath

Boomtime of Chaos
Boomtime of Discord
Boomtime of Confusion
Boomtime of Bureaucracy
Boomtime of Aftermath

Pungenday of Chaos
Pungenday of Discord
Pungenday of Confusion
Pungenday of Bureaucracy
Pungenday of Aftermath

Prickle-Prickle of Chaos
Prickle-Prickle of Discord
Prickle-Prickle of Confusion
Prickle-Prickle of Bureaucracy
Prickle-Prickle of Aftermath

Setting Orange of Chaos
Setting Orange of Discord
Setting Orange of Confusion
Setting Orange of Bureaucracy
Setting Orange of Aftermath

My birthday is September 18, which, on the Discordian calendar, falls on the 42nd day of Confusion. This tells me that my patron saint is Zarathud. Additionally, Confusion 42 falls on Sweetmorn, making my ruling Element Sweet. Ergo, my astrological sign is Sweetmorn of Bureaucracy.

Now, at this point, you may be asking what the individual signs represent, or what personality traits they may characterize. And let me tell you: I have absolutely no idea. This is Discordianism, after all, where things don't have to have a reason for existing, other than for the sake of existing. We can choose to interpret the astrological signs however we'd like, or choose not to interpret them at all, and personally, I think that makes perfect sense.

Then again, I'm a Sweetmorn of Bureaucracy. What else would you expect from me?

Crafting with Chaos
Unverified Personal Tib

St. Tib's Day occurs once every four years and lands between Chaos 59 and 60 (or, in Gregorian terms, on February 29—Leap Year). And, of course, The *Principia* offers a date for St. Tib's Day, with no details on how to celebrate it, let alone any information on who St. Tib was or is.

Ergo, to follow up on Phil Hine's mention of gods that didn't exist five minutes ago, you are going to invent St. Tib.

We can associate St. Tib with fours, since that still aligns with the Law of Fives (four being only one number away from five), and we can assume that Tib is a liminal figure, since Leap Year is kind of a time of no-time. But other than that, what can we conclude about them? That, dear reader, is entirely up to you: You get to build a saint of your very own.

Here are some things to ponder: What is Tib's patronage? What symbols can be associated with Tib? Is "Tib" short for anything? Or is it an acronym? What is Tib's gender? If they're nonbinary, how do they define their gender identity? How does Tib adorn themself? Do they dress ostentatiously, or are they a T-shirt and jeans kind of saint? What would be some appropriate offerings to Tib? Since their feast day only occurs once every four years, when else should Tib be venerated? What would daily devotion to St. Tib look like?

Once you have a perception of St. Tib in mind, craft a short prayer or invocation to them. Cast a five-sided circle as described in chapter 4, call St. Tib into the center of it, and commune with them for a bit. Keep a notebook with you, and write down any impressions or messages you receive. Thank Tib for their presence, and for their decision to exist, before you close the circle.

As a sidenote and/or some inspiration for you: Late one evening, after hours of working feverishly on this manuscript, I fell asleep and had a dream in which there was a sixth Discordian Element called Snooze. If you're in need of a good jumping-off point for your St. Tib veneration, you're more than welcome to steal the idea and associate Snooze with Tib.

Chapter 13
A Miscellany of Misadventures

In looking back over my occult career, I can say with conviction that I've never had a spell not work. I mean, sometimes they didn't quite work as I expected them to, and sometimes they worked far more explosively than anticipated, but every one of them had some kind of impact.

A big part of those impacts was amassed knowledge: The discovery of a new skill, or a self-taught lesson on what to do or not do on the next go-round. It's those lessons that are most important to me, because the Witches around me can learn from them as well.

English novelist Catherin Aird once wrote, "If you can't be a good example, you'll just have to be a horrible warning, that's all."[86] By sharing the experiences I've had with Chaos Witchcraft so far, I get to be much more of the former than the latter. And with that in mind, here are a few of my more memorable exploits.

Of Blood and Sigils

My friend Chester's primary love language is memes, so I always look forward to receiving kooky and

---
86. Aird, *His Burial Too*, 237.

amusing messages from him. Although it did throw me off when he texted one day to ask, "Are you familiar with giving injections in butts?"

"This... feels like a loaded question," I replied.

"Let me rephrase," he texted back. "I'm due for a testosterone shot in the next day or so, but I'm not feeling up to stabbing myself at the moment. Is that something you could help with?"

"Oh, okay," I said. "It's been a while, but sure, I can totally do it."

"That would be excellent, thanks. Doing it myself involves a large mirror and disassociation."

"I worked at a veterinary clinic in high school. I've given a lot of canine booster shots. I can't imagine this being much different."

And it honestly wasn't an unreasonable request. Between Gardnerian Wicca—a practice of which is ritual nudity—and my involvement with the local leather community, I have, at one point or another, seen most of my friends in their birthday suits, so what was one more bum in the grand scheme of things? Plus, I knew that Chester had an aversion to needles, so if administering his injection for him would alleviate his stress, I was happy to do it.

And if he started to panic, I figured I could just do what we did at the vet clinic, and grab him by the scruff of the neck and yell, "Bad dog, no biting," until he settled down.

Which, coincidentally, is also sometimes how we handle things in the leather community. You kind of have to pick your battles.

I went over to Chester's place, and we chitchatted for a while. And once he was ready to take the plunge (so to speak), he shimmied out of his shorts and lay facedown on his bed.

"Here's the syringe," he said.

"Okay."

"And here's an alcohol swab and a Band-Aid."

"Got it."

"And if there's any blood, here's a sigil I printed on tissue paper to absorb it."

"Copy that. Let's do this."

And I jabbed him right in the candy cake.

I watched the injection site for a few seconds, and then I yelled, "We have blood!" And Chester shouted, "Charge it up!" So I dabbed the sigil on the spot until it was good and crimson, and once the flow receded, I applied the Band-Aid and handed Chester the sigil to do whatever else he needed to do with it.

This is one of the things I appreciate most about Chester as a Chaos Magician: When faced with an uncomfortable situation, he looks to see how he can transmute it into something beneficial. In this case, it was, "I am afraid of needles and hate the sight of blood. How can I use that?" And the fear and repulsion became mercurial fuels for his occult operations.

I don't know the purpose of the sigil we charged with his blood, but I don't need to. What I also appreciate is that Chester trusted me to help him without asking unnecessary questions. And since I was able to give him the injection without causing him pain or discomfort, I've been able to help him out with similar workings every week since.

A lot of frowns turned upside down here.

Way back in 1997, former *Chicago Tribune* columnist Mary Schmich advised, "Do one thing every day that scares you," which is excellent advice in general, but even more so for those of us frolicking about in the field of Chaos Magic.[87] And just like how Schmich's "Wear Sunscreen" essay got reworked by Baz Luhrmann into a chart-topping hit single, we can utilize the theories

---

87. Schmich, "Advice, Like Youth, Probably Just Wasted on the Young."

of Chaos Magic to turn pretty much anything into a magical operation.

The Teachable Moment

Can a household chore become a spell? Can data entry be used for divination? Can ingesting a daily medication influence an unrelated spiritual condition or act as metaphysical protection? These are fun questions worth asking, and even if some of the possible answers strike us as kind of daunting, we won't know until we try. So let's try.

Intrusions Will Be Toad

When I was seven years old, I turned on the sink in my bathroom to brush my teeth, unaware that a cockroach roughly the size of a Dodge Caravan was lurking in the basin. The roach went ballistic when hit by the stream of water and flung itself into the air, and I was officially traumatized for life.

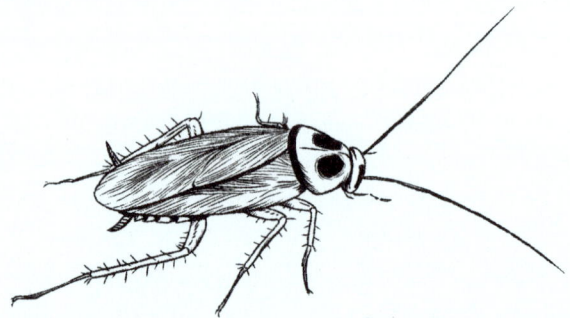

Life-Size Rendition of a Texas Cockroach

Gargantuan roaches are just something you have to come to terms with when you live in the South, even though their sheer size can be a challenge to comprehend. The first time my sister-in-law (she's from Kansas) saw one flying (they fly), she yelled, "Look! A bat!" But as an adult, I decided that I'd had enough of coexistence with eldritch horrors and turned to Witchcraft to deal with the problem. Specifically, I created a servitor to keep roaches out of my apartment. I named him Tygpan Chemdifork, and I am pleased to report that the working was a success. Although getting him up to speed on his duties involved a couple of false starts.

The day after Tygpan was begotten, I wandered into my bathroom to find a midsize roach frantically squeezing itself into the millimeter of space between the vanity mirror and the wall. I was discouraged to see a roach at all, but I also remembered that part of Tygpan's job was to shoo out any six-legged varmints that had already snuck into the apartment. This one was definitely trying to escape from ... something, so I gave Mr. Chemdifork the benefit of the doubt and didn't fuss about it.

The day after that, I came home from work and discovered a very big, very unalive roach lying on its back in the middle of my kitchen floor. There was a subtle sense of pride in the air, similar to that exuded by a cat who's just left a dead mouse on a pillow, and I understood that Tygpan was trying to give me a little trophy to compensate for the previous day's less-than-stellar hunt. So I spoke out loud and told him that I sincerely appreciated the gift, but if he could leave the bodies out of sight from here on out, that would be great.

One more roach appeared in the bathroom about a week later, but this time it was small and easy to eliminate on my own. I called out to Tygpan anyway and explained that even though it was miniscule and easy to let slide under his radar, little roaches grow up to be big roaches, so we needed to make sure to take care of those too.

It was at that moment, standing in front of my toilet and giving a "not angry, just disappointed" lecture to an invisible ball of Pungent and Boom, that I started to wonder if my grip on reality was really as firm as I'd always assumed. But it was also the last time I ever saw a roach around my abode.

Now, there are toads.

On several occasions, I've come home to find a toad standing guard by my doorstep. There is a toad nested under my porch, and toads patrolling the sidewalks of the complex. On one night in particular, I spied two roaches on the bricks outside of my building, but I didn't even twitch, on account of the predatory toad slowly creeping up behind them.

It's almost as if Tygpan was a Pokémon who leveled up from imaginary to amphibious.

Granted, I have no proof that my servitor evolved into a knot of toads, and toads themselves are not without annoyance. They are *loud*, for one thing: Their creaky, high-pitched mating calls are *relentless*. But in the long run, I'd much rather lose sleep because a bunch of toads are feeling randy than because of the crippling fear that the roaches are coming. As long as he continues to chase them away, however Tygpan chooses to incarnate is perfectly fine with me.

The Teachable Moment

Something to think about when casting a spell is *how* you want the results to materialize. I don't mind all the toads—toads are witchy and great—but if I had to do it over, I would have put some limits on how far Tygpan could go to fulfill his insecticidal duties.

The toads undeniably solved my problem, but if any of my neighbors suffer from ranidaphobia—the fear of frogs and toads—I may have caused some unintentional anxiety along with the roach-free relief.

Baphomet Man

By day, I manage an LGBTQ+ leather and fetishwear store, where I've got an employee named Cuttle. Cuttle is a wonderful guy, a hard worker, and a very genuine person—and because some of our customers have (to put it mildly) boundary issues, Cuttle's sincerity sometimes gets misinterpreted.

A customer started coming into the store every day to see Cuttle. Literally every day. He would follow Cuttle around and compliment his tattoos, but he wasn't really causing any problems, and Cuttle didn't seem bothered, so I just decided not to worry about it.

Although he really did come in a lot, and he was *really* into Cuttle's tattoos.

One morning, I showed up to open the store, and I found a plain white envelope slipped under the door. I figured it was an invitation to a neighborhood event or something, but when I opened it, I discovered that it was a typed letter to Cuttle—it started out with a request to turn one of his tattoos into a T-shirt design, but then it just got kind of rambly, and it was signed, Baphomet Man.

While I had no proof it was from that customer, it was... *clearly* from that customer. And here's the thing: If your grammar is not stellar, and you're identifying as Baphomet, there is a fine line between "I want to turn your tattoo into a T-shirt design" and "I want to wear your skin."

Cuttle was completely freaked out by the letter, but I was resolute in my desire to keep him safe. "Listen," I said. "I am not going to let anything bad happen to you." And I started doing protective work around the store with the goal of keeping this guy away from Cuttle. I didn't have much in the way of spell components to work with, but I did find some hand sanitizer and sidewalk chalk, both of which would get the job done.

I sigilized my desire to keep Cuttle free from harm, and I used the chalk to draw that sigil under the rainbow welcome mat in front of our door. And then I went around the store, dabbing the hand sanitizer on any fixture Baphomet Man had touched or leaned against, just to remove the essence of his presence. Finally, I fished around in the drawer under the cash register and pulled out a little rubber ball that Baphomet Man had once left for Cuttle. I grabbed a black marker, drew the sigil onto the ball, then slathered it in the sanitizer (I knew the alcohol in the sanitizer would smear the ink, but in my mind, that was just a manifestation of Baphomet Man's removal), went outside, and chucked it as hard as I could into the vacant lot behind us.

The one thing I didn't have, and desperately needed, was a concrete reason to ban the guy from the store. But I was confident in the magical work I'd done, so I figured everything else would just work itself out. And, most importantly, Cuttle would be safe.

Cuttle and I both had the next day off, but I got a frantic call that morning from my employee on duty, who was weirded out to the point of near aphasia. Apparently, Baphomet Man had come in looking for Cuttle, and when he was told that Cuttle wasn't working, he said, "Oh, I was just going to show him the new drag routine I've been working on. Do you want to see it?"

"I...I guess so?" my employee replied.

At which point Baphomet Man reached under his shirt, where he had concealed two water balloons, and popped them.

To clarify, he exploded water balloons *in a store full of leather*.

My employee had no idea how to react, so he reiterated that Cuttle wouldn't be coming in, waited for Baphomet Man to leave, and then cleaned up the mess. I was on the phone with the store's owners the following morning, explaining the situation and telling them that Baphomet Man was not allowed back in the store.

As soon as I said it, Baphomet Man walked through the door.

"Is Cuttle here?" he asked.

"Did you pop water balloons in my store?" I asked in return.

"Oh, they said I could," he replied.

"In fact, 'they' did not," I shot back. "That was an act of vandalism."

He started to argue, but I cut him off and was like, "Nope. Get out."

"Well, thank you for being polite about this," he said. And he left.

I called the owners back to fill them in on the latest development, and they called the manager of the bar with which we share a building, just to let him know about Baphomet Man as well. To which the manager responded, "What a coincidence! We just banned him from our establishment, for completely unrelated reasons."

And none of us ever saw him again. But I do appreciate that in doing work to protect Cuttle, I was granted a solid reason to keep Baphomet Man away from all of us.

The Teachable Moment

This is just how Chaos Witchcraft seems to operate at times. The results of your spells may not be quite what you'd foretold when you cast them, but you will get results nonetheless.

Welcome to the Ellis, Said the Spider to the Witch

Tuesdays are traditionally slow in retail, so I spent the morning reading about the history of the Domus Khaotica Marauder Underground. I was intrigued by some of the capers they'd pulled off—specifically, one in which a couple of early members designed a sigil to link areas of magical power together, creating a web that any practitioner could theoretically access to boost their own workings.

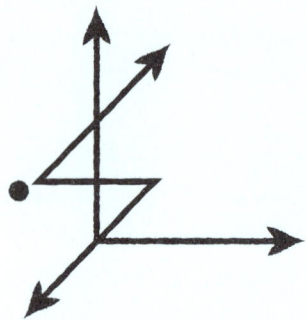

The Linking Sigil

The DKMU writings suggested that the Linking Sigil, or Ellis (LS), could be placed at any location significant for its sanctity, metaphysical resonance, or liminality. In my mind, a minority-owned business catering to a subculture within a subculture is pretty darn liminal, so I figured that plugging the store into the Ellis network would definitely be keeping in line with the sigil's intent.

Inspired, I ran outside to draw the Ellis in silver Sharpie upon a large pebble next to the store's front stoop. And as they say, bad decisions make great stories—as such, I was completely at peace with everything that happened next.

Day 1

Customers started trickling in about ten minutes after I inscribed the sigil, and they spent a surprising amount of money, as did the customers who came in after them. By the time a coworker showed up to relieve me, we'd beaten all sales for previous Tuesdays and were well on our way to setting a weekday record.

I was working a split shift and ended up with a couple of hours to kill, so I messaged Chester to see what he was doing. "I'm just hanging out at my place," he replied. "Want to come by and let me zap you with a New Age gadget to decalcify your pineal gland?"

Two hours later, freshly ascended, I went back to the store, where I found my very bored coworker waiting for me.

"It's been dead since you left," he said. "Literally no one has come in."

As soon as those words left his mouth, the door flew open, and a customer bounded in.

"Hello!" he exclaimed. "I have never been here before and aim to do some shopping!" The whole thing was eerily similar to that scene in *Little Shop of Horrors*, where some guy who may or may not be an alien can't help noticing that strange and interesting plant in the flower shop window and then buys one hundred dollars' worth of roses. And I myself couldn't help noticing that sales for the day seemed directly tied to my presence.

Day 2

My boss asked me to come in an hour early, which put me comfortably into overtime. The first customer of the day seemed very polite, but every time my boss left the room, he aggressively hit on me: It was very Doctor Jekyll and Daddy Hyde. He eventually made some purchases and left, right as the phone rang. The caller explained that a friend had sent him some ... playthings, and he wasn't sure how to use them. Could I talk him through that in explicit detail?

Raising my voice slightly so as to drown out his heavy breathing, I told him that I unfortunately could not be of assistance and ended the call. Perfect timing, as it turned out, because customers were piling in, and a disquieting number of them took unusual interest in me. But it was also another day of underestimated profit, so I called it even.

Day 3

"Would you be willing to choke me? It helps with my PTSD."

The customer understood when I declined, and he bought a bunch of stuff anyway. But it was pretty much a representative sample of all the interactions throughout my shift. Sales were once again brisk, although my tolerance for boundary issues was beginning to wear thin.

What finally did me in, though, was the spider hiding in the upper reaches of our covered porch, who waited patiently until I stepped out front to get some air, then gleefully repelled down from the rafters a few inches from my face.

I'm pretty sure there were no witnesses, so I can say with a straight face that I did *not* scream like a twelve-year-old at a Taylor Swift concert. And apparently, a lot of practitioners who've scratched the surface of the Linking Sigil have sensed or actually met an intelligence within its connected matrix. Some have described this presence as a middle-aged, red-haired woman identified as Ellis herself (who may or may not also be Eris), while others report brushes with a character resembling the protagonist from *Alice in Wonderland*. And some just say it's a big spider.

I live in Texas. We have spiders. And I refuse to ascribe spiritual import to any and every chance encounter with wildlife. But I will say that after seventy-two hours of gainful strangeness, getting ambushed by what may or may not have been Ellis herself was enough to make me bring the experiment to a close.

Having gleaned some insight into the sigil and its capabilities, I ritually severed my link to the network. And by that, I mean I ritually took the pebble out to the parking lot and ritually demolished it with a hammer.

According to the DKMU, drawing the Ellis without any purpose behind it will bring chaos (not the good kind), whereas drawing the sigil with a specific goal in mind will trigger successful but unexpected results. Considering the events of those three days, I can confirm this with aplomb. And I do plan on working more with Ellis, just in an environment with fewer variables.

Sales dipped mildly after I smashed the pebble, but my customers went back to being pleasant and emotionally distant. I took both as strong signs that any other ingenious, work-related woo I devise should be placed directly on the non-sentient register.

The Teachable Moment

If I'd done a little more research on the Linking Sigil, I would have exercised more caution before doodling it on rocks. Don't be afraid to experiment, but do make sure you have all the information you need before fumbling around and finding out. Creepy customers may not always be worth the magical outcome.

Cassandra Pleads the Fifth

A metaphysical shop not too far from me hosts a Psychic Sunday event twice a month, and I'm on their rotating roster of prognosticators. So, once every six weeks or so, I get to spend my afternoon hanging out in a cozy, magical space and offering lithomantic readings to the general public.

It's a rewarding experience overall, although I do seem to attract more than my fair share of what I've come to call jump scare clients. These are people who have specific questions in mind, but they're not willing to lead with them. Instead, they test the waters, making sure they're comfortable with me and what I have to say. They pitch a few innocuous queries and give me a false sense of security, then pull a 180 and shank me with the heavy stuff.

"I just want a general reading," they say, "Maybe about...oh, I don't know, love? Or money?" And then, fifteen minutes later, they're leaning over the table between us like, "How much prison time am I looking at, exactly?" and the tarot reader in the booth next to mine stops shuffling.

I've learned to operate under the assumption that *any* client could be a potential jump scare, although every once in a while, one of them manages to catch me off guard. Like a particular gentleman for whom I've read several times, who normally only comes in with questions about his various business ventures. He turned up one Sunday with standard inquiries in tow, but after we'd covered the usual fare (do invest in futures; do not sell the truck), he palmed a curveball out of nowhere and winged it at me.

"So...I have this friend," he said. "She's currently in the hospital, and she won't tell me what's going on, but I'm worried about her, and I just want to know if she's okay."

It was a fair, unintrusive question, albeit an unexpected divergence from his normal requests. But it also would only require a simple yes or no, so I gathered up my stones and gave them a toss, watching as one of them hit the casting cloth at a funny angle and bounced right out of the circle.

I didn't realize I was staring at the stone until several awkward seconds later, when the client cleared his throat and asked, "Does that...does that mean anything?"

"If a stone lands outside of the circle, it's irrelevant to the reading," I explained, composing myself. And that is almost always true—except sometimes, when a stone deliberately removes itself, it has a story all its own to relate. In this case, I suddenly had insight into why his friend went to the hospital, and what she had done, and why she wasn't talking to him about it. It was like the stone was a Pokémon ball, but instead of a charming little monster, some random stranger's medical history popped out.

It was a lot of information that he hadn't asked for, and that I wasn't comfortable holding. But because he didn't ask, there was no reason for me to point any of it out to him. Instead, I dragged my eyes over the rest of the reading. Death next to Pungent and Thinking, Wealth near Prickle and Boom: No, she would not be talking about it, but yes, she would indeed be okay.

When it comes to lithomancy, I'm right more often than I'm wrong, and I trust my ability to interpret what the stones are trying to say. But sometimes, when more pistons are firing than can feasibly fit in my engine, my gears inevitably shift toward, "You know, this is just a disorderly scattering of rocks. They mean nothing. There is no logic behind this. Do not believe anything that comes out of my mouth." There is an upside, though, to getting bludgeoned by a lithomantic info dump, in that it tells me there's more going on than the client is sharing. Which in turn gives me tools to direct the rest of the reading.

The Teachable Moment

When divining for other people, do your best to stick with clear yes-no answers, and don't wander too far off course. In turn, the person for whom you are reading won't be encouraged to ask about things they don't really want or need to know. And that lets both of you off the hook.

Conclusion

"The Parable of Steve" is not part of the *Principia Discordia*—rather, it appeared in the later anthology *Et Cetera Discordia*—but it has become a beloved piece of Discordian lore.

Following is my attempt at retelling it.

One afternoon, this guy named Steve was browsing at his local independent bookstore, when he came across a copy of the *Principia Discordia*. He flipped through a few pages and was like, "This is *it*. This is the answer! I'm rebellious, and anti-authority, and I have a great sense of humor, and I appreciate the absurd: I am … *Discordian*."

And he set off to find other Discordians.

He also renamed himself Pope Buttercup the 23rd.

Eventually, Steve learned that a local Discordian society met monthly at a nearby coffee shop, so on the day of the meetup, he charged into the venue, ready to be embraced by his tribe. But the place was empty, except for a group of people in a booth in the back corner. And these were, like, nondescript, everyday people—one of them was wearing a business suit, and another looked like she could be somebody's grandma.

But they were aggressively arguing with each other, so Steve was like, "Hmm. These are probably the Discordians." He marched up to the table and loudly announced, "Twenty-three pineal fnord! I am Pope Buttercup the 23rd! I am random! I say random things! And I am a Discordian like you!"[88]

And everyone at the table looked at him for a second, and then they went back to arguing.

So Steve tried again.

"Pardon me," he said, toning it down a little this time. "But could you tell me where the monkeys fly at midnight? Modern politics bore me, and I can swallow my own nose!"

At this point, Steve realized that a few of the people at the table had started making fun of him. Like, they were pointing at him, and whispering to each other and laughing.

And this *infuriated* Steve. He was like, "Hey! I'm the real Discordian here! You're just like everyone else! You're supposed to be *different*. You should be paying attention to *me*, and listening to *me*, so that *I* can teach *you* how to be Discordian!"

To prove his point, Steve started dancing around and yelling the most absurd things he could think of while squawking like a chicken.

"I am the paulrus," he shouted. "Together we turntable the green otter! Buck-*bawk*!"

And the table erupted. One third of the group started yelling back at Steve and telling him to leave them alone; a second third of the group started yelling at the first third, telling *them* to shut up and leave Steve alone; and the third third just kept trying to keep their original conversation going, but they couldn't hear each other over all the commotion.

---

88. Nigel, "The Parable of Steve," 00073.

Finally, a barista stormed over to the table and was like, "What the actual hell is going on over here?!"

Everyone stopped yelling. And then, the quietest member of the group looked up at the barista and whispered, "Discord."

The overarching message is that there is no One True Way to practice Discordianism, just like there's no One True Way to practice Chaos Witchcraft—trying to cram it into a unified box is just applying Destructive Order to Creative Disorder, which inevitably results in Destructive Disorder. Instead, our unity comes from our differences, and the celebration of those differences. As Mal-2 once said, "We Discordians must stick apart."

There is no right way to be a Chaos Witch, and there never will be. There's only *your* way.

A Decade of Discord

Per the Discordian calendar, *Et Cetera Discordia* was published in 3175, fifty years after the first publication of the *Principia Discordia*, whereas the majority of *The Chaos Apple* was written in 3189. However, according to the Gregorian calendar, the year was 2023, and since twenty-three is a sacred Discordian number, the next decade officially belongs to Eris—her reign will end on December 31, 2032.

And honestly, Gregorians have no one but themselves to blame for that. Quoth the grand folks over at PrincipiaDiscordia.com on the matter, "Buckle up."

As with almost everything else within Discordianism, we aren't even teased with a hint as to what we're supposed to do with this information, or how we might prepare for a decade of Erisian mischief. I feel like it's safe(?) to say that the Discordian seasons will be more pronounced, with Chaos, Discord, Confusion,

Bureaucracy, and Aftermath all living up to their names. So that's definitely something against which to gird your loins.

Although speaking of names: In honor of the Era of Eris, 2023 was the year I added Horkos to my already way-too-long nom de plume.

As mentioned earlier, Horkos is the Greek personification of curses against those who break oaths. He's also the only child of Eris who's not an unrepentant savage, so incorporating His name into my own (probably) won't bring unnecessary horrors into my life. Additionally, this gives me five names instead of four—Thumper Όρκος Marjorie Splitfoot Forge—with a grand total of ten syllables. Plus *hork* is one of the funniest words in the English language, so yeah. Discordian as all get-out.

But most importantly, in a Discordian worldview, the one most likely to break oaths is Greyface, so it is against him that Horkos rages. And since, as Chaos Witches, it is up to us to throw as many Turkey Curses as we can at Greyface and his Aneristic retinue, we are all Horkos as well.

Granted, making my name even harder to fit on my debit card won't save me or anyone else from a one-hundred-twenty-month onslaught of Disorder. We're going to have to pick our battles as we wade through bimodalities of weirdness, focusing as much as we can on the Creative instead of granting power to the Destructive.

Once Upon an Apple

Here's another parable on this very subject—a fable by Aesop this time—with a moral worth minding as we stumble forward for the next ten years and beyond.

Many moons ago, in the romantic utopia that is mythological Greece, Heracles was wandering down a narrow road when he spotted an apple in his path. Miffed by the tiny obstacle, he attempted to smash it with his heel, on account of ... he had an allergy? Hated carbs? Aesop wasn't clear on this part.

Anyway, Heracles stomped on the apple, and it promptly inflated to twice its size. He stomped on it repeatedly, but it just kept growing larger. Finally, he tried hitting it with his club, at which point the apple expanded so massively that it completely blocked his path.

Heracles was standing there, glaring helplessly at this kaiju of a fruit, when Athena suddenly appeared next to him.

"What's up?" she asked.

Fully enraged by then, Heracles just gestured violently at the gargantuan apple and did that mouth-flapping thing that happens when you're too angry to form coherent words.

"Ah, I see," said Athena, translating. "That right there is the Apple of Discord. Ask me how I know. If you don't mess with it, it stays small; but if you try to fight it, it swells into something unmanageable."

"Like a sebaceous cyst?" Heracles asked.

"I mean ... sure, okay," Athena replied, recalling why she avoided cameos in his myths. "Exactly like that. But if you'll excuse me, I gotta be somewhere else. Like, immediately. Goddess of wisdom stuff."

Destructive Order begets Destructive Disorder, and the angrier we get about not being able to control, say, inevitable inconveniences, or arguments on the internet, the more uncontrollable those things become. Better to let sleeping apples lie in the road and direct our attention to the issues that *are* within our capacity to manage. Like how we react to those obstacles when we encounter them.

Page 00074 of the *Principia Discordia* offers a similar, if slightly more differently sane, take on the situation:

> The human race will begin solving its problems on the day that it ceases taking itself so seriously.
>
> If you can master nonsense as well as you have already learned to master sense, then each will expose the other for what it is: absurdity. From that moment of illumination, a man begins to be free regardless of his surroundings. He becomes free to play order games and change them at will. He becomes free to play disorder games just for the hell of it. He becomes free to play neither or both. And as the master of his own games, he plays without fear, and therefore without frustration, and therefore with good will in his soul and love in his being.

No matter what inanities get thrown at us, we will undoubtedly thrive and survive, provided we keep in mind that humor is just as important as seriousness, and that laughter transcends all other emotions. The more fun we can have, the more empowered we'll be—after all, the winner is always the one who laughs last.

Happy Decade of Our Lady Discordia, my fellow Clown Witches and Chaotes. Go off and joyously partake of a hotdog. You've earned it.

Chaos Continued

I've mentioned quite a number of books throughout *The Chaos Apple*, most notably *Liber Null & Psychonaut* by Peter J. Carroll, *Condensed Chaos* by Phil Hine, and of course the *Principia Discordia*. But there are thousands of manuals, grimoires, and fictional works out there that can guide you as you come into your own as a Chaos Witch.

Following are a variety of resources that were incredibly helpful to me on my own Chaos Witchcraft journey, categorized by subject. I am confident that they will prove useful to you as well.

Chaos Magical Theory

Channing, Anton. *Kaos Hieroglyphica*. Mandrake, 2003.

Hawkins, Jaq D. *The Chaonomicon: Quintessential Chaos for the Serious Magician*. Independently published, 2018.

Humphries, Greg, and Julian Vayne. *Now That's What I Call Chaos Magick*. Mandrake, 2005.

Sherwin, Ray. *The Theatre of Magick*. Lulu.com, 2006.

Smith, Leonard. *Chaos: A Very Short Introduction*. Oxford University Press, 2007.

Discordianism

Black, Edwin. *Kallisti: A Discordian Tale*. Independently published, 2019.

Clutterbuck, Brenton. *Chasing Eris*. Lulu.com, 2018.

Cramulus and LMNO. *The Chao Te Ching*. Lulu.com, 2011.

Discordia, Eris Kallisti. *The Book of Eris*. Lulu.com, 2006.

Gorightly, Adam. *The Prankster and the Conspiracy: The Story of Kerry Thornley and How He Met Oswald and Inspired the Counterculture*. Paraview Press, 2003.

Witchcraft

Kelden. *The Crooked Path: An Introduction to Traditional Witchcraft*. Llewellyn Publications, 2020.

Mankey, Jason. *The Witch's Book of Spellcraft: A Practical Guide to Connecting with the Magick of Candles, Crystals, Plants & Herbs*. Llewellyn Publications, 2022.

Mooney, Thorn. *The Witch's Path: Advancing Your Craft at Every Level*. Llewellyn Publications, 2011.

Orapello, Christopher, and Tara-Love Maguire. *Besom, Stang & Sword: A Guide to Traditional Witchcraft, the Six-Fold Path & the Hidden Landscape*. Weiser Books, 2018.

Rajchel, Diana. *Urban Magick: A Guide for the City Witch*. Llewellyn Publications, 2020.

Greek Religion and Mythology

Gooch, Brad. *Dating the Greek Gods: Empowering Spiritual Messages on Sex and Love, Creativity and Wisdom*. Simon and Schuster, 2003.

Hekataios, Oracle. *Strix Craft: Ancient Greek Magic for the Modern Witch*. Crossed Crow Books, 2025.

Mankey, Jason, and Astrea Taylor. *Modern Witchcraft with the Greek Gods: History, Insights & Magickal Practice*. Llewellyn Publications, 2022.

Miller, Madeline. *Circe*. Back Bay Books, 2020.

O'Brien, Corey. *Zeus Grants Stupid Wishes: A No-Bullshit Guide to World Mythology*. TarcherPerigee, 2013.

Sigils and Servitors

Brand, Damon. *Magickal Servitors: Create Your Own Spirits to Attract Pleasure, Power and Prosperity*. CreateSpace Independent Publishing, 2016.

Fries, Jan. *Visual Magick: A Manual of Freestyle Shamanism*. Mandrake, 2007.

Wachter, Aiden. *Weaving Fate: Hypersigils, Changing the Past, & Telling True Lies*. Ygret Niche Publishing, 2020.

Zakroff, Laura Tempest. *Sigil Witchery: A Witch's Guide to Crafting Magick Symbols*. Llewellyn Publications, 2018.

Zakroff, Laura Tempest. *Visual Alchemy: A Witch's Guide to Sigils, Art & Magic*. Llewellyn Publications, 2022.

Creative Disorder

Gore, Ariel. *Hexing the Patriarchy: 26 Potions, Spells, and Magical Elixirs to Embolden the Resistance*. Seal Press, 2019.

Lipp, Deborah. *Bending the Binary: Polarity Magic in a Nonbinary World*. Llewellyn Publications, 2023.

Quinn, Daniel. *The Story of B*. Bantam, 1997.

Salisbury, David. *Witchcraft Activism: A Toolkit for Magical Resistance*. Weiser Books, 2019.

Thornley, Kerry W. *Zenarchy*. IllumiNet Press, 1991.

Spirituality

Dee, Steve. *Chaos Monk: Bringing Magical Creativity to the New Monastic Path*. The Universe Machine, 2022.

Frater Tenebris. *The Philosophy of Dark Paganism: Wisdom and Magick to Cultivate the Self*. Llewellyn Publications, 2022.

Hebert, Deidre A. *The Pagan in Recovery: The Twelve Steps from a Pagan Perspective*. Asphodel Press, 2011.

Higginbotham, Vincent. *How Witchcraft Saved My Life: Practical Advice for Transformative Magick*. Llewellyn Publications, 2021.

Matthey, Moss. *An Apostate's Guide to Witchcraft: Finding Freedom Through Magic*. Llewellyn Publications, 2024.

Divination and Astrology

Bills, Rex E. *The Rulership Book*. American Federation of Astrologers, 2007.

DuQuette, Lon Milo. *The Book of Ordinary Oracles: Use Pocket Change, Popsicle Sticks, a TV Remote, This Book, and More to Predict the Future and Answer Your Questions*. Weiser Books, 2005.

Le Grice, Keiron. *Discovering Eris: The Symbolism and Significance of a New Planetary Archetype*. Floris Books, 2012.

Saint Germain, Jon. *Lithomancy: Divination and Spellcraft with Stones, Crystals, and Coins*. Lucky Mojo Curio Company, 2018.

Zakroff, Laura Tempest. *Liminal Spirits Oracle*. Llewellyn Publications, 2020.

Bibliography

Adler, Margot. *Drawing Down the Moon: Witches, Druids, Goddess-Worshippers, and Other Pagans in America Today (Revised and Expanded Edition)*. Beacon Press, 1986.

Aesop. *The Complete Fables*. Translated by Olivia and Robert Temple. Penguin Classics, 1998.

Agrippa, Henry Cornelius. *The Fourth Book of Occult Philosophy: The Companion to Three Books of Occult Philosophy*. Translated by Robert Turner. Llewellyn Publications, 2009.

Aird, Catherian. *His Burial Too*. Open Road Media Mystery & Thriller, 2015.

Atsma, Aaron J. "Eris." Theoi Project. Accessed December 5, 2023. https://theoi.com/Daimon/Eris.html.

Atsma, Aaron J. "Horkos." Theoi Project. Accessed December 15, 2023. https://theoi.com/Daimon/Eris.html.

Babcock, Jay. "Magic Is Afoot: A Conversation with Alan Moore About the Arts and the Occult." *Arthur*, no. 4. Floating World Comics, 2003.

Belanger, M. *The Dictionary of Demons*. Llewellyn Publications, 2024.

Bey, Hakim. *T.A.Z.: The Temporary Autonomous Zone, Ontological Anarchy, Poetic Terrorism*. Autonomedia, 2003.

Blome, Karactus J. *Magia Proelio Discordia: The Final Magnum Opiate of Alynaar the Shattered*. CreateSpace Independent Publishing, 2017.

Bring It On. Directed by Peyton Reed. Paramount Pictures, 2000.

Buckland, Raymond. *The Magick of Chant-O-Matics*. Parker Publishing, 1982.

Buckland, Raymond. *Scottish Witchcraft: The History & Magick of the Picts*. Llewellyn Publications, 2003.

Carroll, Peter J. *Liber Null & Psychonaut: An Introduction to Chaos Magic*. Weiser Books, 1987.

Carroll, Peter J. *Liber Kaos*. Weiser Books, 1992.

Carter, Maria. "Why Does Easter Change Dates? Here's How the Date Is Determined." *Country Living*, January 23, 2024.

"Chaos Magick Involves Drugs, Orgies & Going Insane." YouTube. Uploaded by Kelly-Ann Maddox, February 1, 2016. https://youtu.be/Vpr8OvofZ9w?si=FDgdiHRP66IF9ah0.

"Chapter Twenty-Six: All of Them Witches." *Chilling Adventures of Sabrina*. Created by Roberto Aguirre-Sacasa. Season 3, episode 6. Warner Bros. Television, 2020.

Clements, Frederic E. *Plant Succession and Indicators*. Hafner, 1928.

Cline, Eric H., and Glynnis Fawkes. *1177 B.C.: A Graphic History of the Year Civilization Collapsed: Revised and Updated*. Princeton University Press, 2021.

Clueless. Directed by Amy Heckerling. Paramount Pictures, 1995.

Cramulus, editor. *Et Cetera Discordia: The Party at Limbo Peak: New Iterations of the Discordian Fractal*. Lulu.com, 2010.

Crowther, Patricia. *Lid Off the Cauldron: A Handbook for Witches*. Frederick Muller, 1981.

The Craft. Directed by Alan Flemming. Columbia Pictures, 1996.

Cusack, Carole. "Discordian Magic: Paganism, the Chaos Paradigm and the Power of Parody." *International Journal for the Study of New Religions* 2.1. Equinox Publishing, 2011.

Darby, Conley. *Get Fuzzy*. United Feature Syndicate, 2007.

DKMU. *Liber LS: Volume One*. CreateSpace Independent Publishing, 2016.

Dominguez, Ivo, Jr., and Thumper Forge. *Virgo Witch: Divining the Details*. Llewellyn Publications, 2023.

Dukes, Ramsey. *Uncle Ramsey's Little Book of Demons: The Positive Advantages of the Personification of Life's Problems*. Aeon Books, 2005.

Eddington, Arthur. *The Nature of the Physical World*. University of Michigan Press, 1981.

Edward, Ryan. *Maybe Lenormand*. U.S. Games Systems, 2016.

Fitzpatrick, Waspie Joanne. *Chaos Covens and Chaos Witchcraft in Practice*. https://zenodo.org/records/12743378.

Gaiman, Neil. *American Gods*. William Morrow, 2001.

Gorightly, Adam. *Historia Discordia*. Rvp Press, 2014.

Greene, Heather. *Lights, Camera, Witchcraft: A Critical History of Witches in American Film and Television*. Llewellyn Publications, 2021.

"Hand of Glory." Whitby Museum. Accessed November 23, 2024. https://whitbymuseum.org.uk/hand-of-glory/.

Hesiod. *Theogony, Works and Days, and the Shield of Heracles*. Translated by Hugh G. Evelyn-White. Digireads.com Publishing, 2018.

Higgs, John. *The KLF: Chaos, Magic and the Band Who Burned a Million Pounds*. Wedenfeld & Nicolson, 2012.

Hill, Greg, and Kerry Thornley. *Principia Discordia or How I Found Goddess and What I Did to Her When I Found Her: The Magnum Opiate of Malaclypse the Younger, Wherein Is Explained Absolutely Everything Worth Knowing About Absolutely Anything*. 4th ed. KopyLeft, All Rites Reversed, 1970.

Hine, Phil. *Condensed Chaos: An Introduction to Chaos Magic*. The Original Falcon Press, 2010.

Hine, Phil. *Oven-Ready Chaos*. Chaos Matrix, 1992. http://www.chaosmatrix.org/library/chaos/texts/orchaos.pdf.

Howard, Jessica. *Pagan Portals—The Art of Lithomancy: Divination with Stones, Crystals, and Charms*. Moon Books, 2022.

Huson, Paul. *Mastering Witchcraft: A Practical Guide for Witches, Warlocks & Covens*. G. P. Putnam's Sons, 1971.

Johnson, Steve. *The Callipygian Grimoire: A Discordian Activity and Spell Book*. CreateSpace Independent Publishing, 2015.

Jurassic Park. Directed by Steven Spielberg. Universal Pictures, 1993.

Kaldera, Raven, and Tannin Schwartzstein. *The Urban Primitive: Paganism in the Concrete Jungle*. Llewellyn Publications, 2002.

KAOS. Created by Charlie Covell. Season 1, episode 8. Anthem Productions, 2024.

King, Stephen. *Everything's Eventual: 14 Dark Tales*. Scribner, 2002.

Lipp, Deborah. "Thoughts on Motherhood." *Property of a Lady* (blog), May 13, 2007. http://www.deborahlipp.com/2007/05/thoughts-on-motherhood/.

Little Shop of Horrors. Directed by Frank Oz. The Geffen Company, 1986.

Lyons, Sarah. *Revolutionary Witchcraft: A Guide to Magical Activism*. Running Press Adult, 2019.

Maddox, Kelly-Ann. *Rebel Witch: Carve the Craft That's Yours Alone*. Watkins Publishing, 2021.

Mankey, Jason, and Astraea Taylor. *Modern Witchcraft with the Greek Gods*. Llewellyn Publications, 2022.

Matthews, Caitlín. *The Complete Lenormand Oracle Handbook: Reading the Language and Symbols of the Cards*. Destiny Books, 2014.

McMillan, Tracy. *I Love You and I'm Leaving You Anyway: A Memoir*. It Books, 2010.

McNally, Terrence. *A Perfect Ganesh*. Random House, 1993.

Metzger, Richard, editor. *Book of Lies: The Disinformation Guide to Magick and the Occult*. Disinformation Books, 2014.

Michael, Coby. *The Poison Path Herbal: Baneful Herbs, Medicinal Nightshades, and Ritual Ethnogens*. Inner Traditions/Bear & Company, 2021.

Miéville, China. *Kraken*. Del Rey Books, 2010.

Moore, Alan. *Promethea: 20th Anniversary Deluxe Edition (Books One, Two, and Three)*. Vertigo, 2019.

Moreno, Carolina. "Portland Burrito Cart Closes After Owners Are Accused of Cultural Appropriation." *HuffPost*, May 25, 2017. https://www.huffpost.com/entry/portland-burrito-cart-closes-after-owners-are-accused-of-cultural-appropriation_n_5926ef7ee4b062f96a348181.

Morrison, Grant. "Pop Magic!" In *Book of Lies: The Disinformation Guide to Magick and the Occult*. Edited by Richard Metzger. Disinformation Books, 2014.

Nigel. "The Parable of Steve." In *Et Cetera Discordia: The Party at Limbo Peak: New Iterations of the Discordian Fractal*. Lulu.com, 2010.

Papadopoulos, Renos K. *The Handbook of Jungian Psychology: Theory, Practice and Applications*. Routledge, 2006.

Pintado, Amanda Pérez. "Twitter Blue Parody Accounts Flood the Platform After New Subscription Service Rollout." *USA Today*, November 14, 2022.

Practical Magic. Directed by Griffin Dunne. Village Roadshow Pictures, 1998.

Pratchett, Terry. *The Colour of Magic*. Harper Paperbacks, 2024.

Regius, Codex. *Lucian vs. the False Prophet: Translation and Annotations*. CreateSpace Independent Publishing, 2017.

Roger, Jolly. "About the DKMU." *Liber LS: Volume One*. CreateSpace Independent Publishing, 2016.

Schmich, Mary. "Advice, Like Youth, Probably Just Wasted on the Young." *Chicago Tribune*, June 1, 1997.

Schwartz, Alvin, and Glen Rounds. *Cross Your Fingers, Spit in Your Hat: Superstitions and Other Beliefs*. Trophy Pr, 1993.

Shamen. "Re:Evolution." *Boss Drum*. One Little Independent Records, 1992.

Sherwin, Ray. *The Book of Results*. Lulu.com, 2010.

Smith, Clark Ashton. "The Empire of the Necromancer." *Weird Tales: A Magazine of the Bizarre and Unusual* 20, no. 3 (September 1932).

Spritedust. "Glamourbomb." Urban Dictionary. Accessed April 30, 2025. https://www.urbandictionary.com/define.php?term=glamourbomb.

Starhawk. *The Spiral Dance: A Rebirth of the Ancient Religion of the Goddess: 20th Anniversary Edition*. HarperOne, 1999.

Summers, Montague. *Witchcraft and Black Magic*. Courier Dover Publications, 2012.

Svendsen, Lea. *Loki and Sigyn: Lessons on Chaos, Laughter & Loyalty from the Norse Gods*. Llewellyn Publications, 2022.

Thornley, Kerry, and Roldo Odlor. *Goetia Discordia: Kerry Thornley's Illustrated Book of the Demons of the Region of Thud*. Bathtub Books, 2017.

"The Total Film Interview—Jodie Foster." *GameRadar+*, December 1, 2005. https://www.gamesradar.com/the-total-film-interview-jodie-foster/.

Updike, John. *The Witches of Eastwick*. Alfred A. Knopf, 1984.

Valiente, Doreen. *Witchcraft for Tomorrow*. Phoenix Publishing, 1978.

Vayne, Julian, and Steve Dee. *Chaos Craft: The Wheel of the Year in Eight Colors*. The Universe Machine, 2016.

W., Bill. *Alcoholics Anonymous*. 4th ed. Alcoholics Anonymous World Services, 2002.

Wein, Len, and Dave Cockrum. *Giant-Size X-Men #1*. Marvel Comics, 1975.

The Wicker Man. Directed by Robin Hardy. British Lion Films, 1973.

Wilson, Robert Anton, and Robert Shea. *The Illuminatus! Trilogy: The Eye in the Pyramid, The Golden Apple, Leviathan*. Dell Books, 1983.

To Write to the Author

If you wish to contact the author or would like more information about this book, please write to the author in care of Llewellyn Worldwide Ltd. and we will forward your request. Both the author and the publisher appreciate hearing from you and learning of your enjoyment of this book and how it has helped you. Llewellyn Worldwide Ltd. cannot guarantee that every letter written to the author can be answered, but all will be forwarded. Please write to:

Thumper Forge
℅ Llewellyn Worldwide
2143 Wooddale Drive
Woodbury, MN 55125-2989

Please enclose a self-addressed stamped envelope for reply,
or $1.00 to cover costs. If outside the U.S.A., enclose
an international postal reply coupon.

Many of Llewellyn's authors have websites with additional information and resources. For more information, please visit our website at http://www.llewellyn.com.